Jim Stewart
The 909

The 909 area code is a classic example of area code proliferation in California. The 909 area code, which includes cities and communities in parts of the counties of Riverside, San Bernardino, and Los Angeles, was implemented in 1992 when it was geographically split from the 714 area code. The 714 area code was created in 1951, when it was split from the 213 area code, one of the three original area codes assigned to California in 1948.

- From the California Public Utilities Commission Website

Equity Press
5055 Canyon Crest Drive
Riverside, CA 92507

This book is a work of fiction. Names, places, and incidents either are products of the author's imagination or are used fictitiously. Any resemblance to actual events or locales or persons, living or dead, is entirely coincidental.

Copyright © 2003 by Jim Stewart

All rights reserved including the right of reproduction in whole or in part in any form.

Cover Design by Eddy Guitierrez
Initial design and concept by Tony Wang

Please visit our website at
www.909thebook.com

ISBN 0-975-30523-9

This book is for Frank, Michele, and Marianne

"You sold out a long time ago, Darling." – in an email from Rebecca Shoenkopf, OC Weekly's Commie Girl.

"If I were interviewing you, I'd put that in the interview." – in conversation with Rolling Stone's Alison Rosen – she wasn't interviewing me at the time.

"Do you think you're going to die young?" – in an interview with KUCR's DJ Tina Bold.

"What happened to you, man? Weren't you born in Orange County?" – in conversation with *Super Steve Florez* of KROQ radio's *Kevin and Bean* morning radio show.

"Riverside is the gem of my ass. " KROQ's Kevin

"So what do you like about living in Riverside?" –Janet Wilson, Los Angeles Times

PART ONE

PART ONE

CHAPTER ONE

David Grey graduated first in his class from the Los Angeles Police Department academy. Don't think that this impresses me much as a professional credential, but it meant a lot to David. Actually I don't think he liked police work all that much, but he learned to be a good cop to battle the inferiority complex he had gotten from being unpopular in high school. There was a certain inner comfort in knowing that he could detain, arrest, and even shoot a person anytime he wanted to. Still being pretty decent kid, he never did shoot anyone. He was his academy sergeant's star trainee. David's academy sergeant taught all of his new recruits to be tough and assertive and unflinchingly rigid in their scrutiny of suspects. And the rigidity and toughness and black and white moral code of a cop seemed to fit Grey, who was a pretty smart guy but was really very naive. It wasn't up to him to interpret the laws, just enforce them. David turned out to be such a good cop that his sergeant assigned him to ride along one night on a drug bust that got him shot in the throat. This increased Grey's distaste for police work but gave him a badge of honor, and it gave him an affinity towards anything in a turtleneck. In his last year at the academy he studied the California penal code too much and started to wear glasses. I never met anyone in the LAPD who remembered him. They didn't even remember that he graduated at the top of his class.

I don't like cops. Especially because they are trained to lie in order to you to get you to admit to a crime, and I always figured that maybe David was lying about graduating first in his academy class, and that he really shot himself at the target range or that maybe his dad shot him as a kid, but I was finally able to get the story verified through a DA that knew his academy sergeant. His academy sergeant remembered who he was and asked how he was doing.

David Grey was a member of a very middle class family and growing up both of his parents worked as elementary school teachers. No one had ever made him conscious of being poor, and no one had made him conscious of his lower socioeconomic status. Sometimes he was brash and abrasive and he lacked the social graces and clothes of the more affluent kids, but he was basically a good guy. No one had ever made him feel poor or lacking in any way until he was a cop, and while he was at the academy he met lawyers, doctors, and businesspeople with money, class, and status. He was a good enough guy, but sometimes he was awkward and very middle class and it ultimately made him bitter towards people with money and toward society in general. He took it out in his police work, and he came out of the academy with a very big chip on his

THE 909

shoulder, a bullet wound in his neck, and he married the first girl that he fell in love with.

After three years of marriage and two kids, he spent or lost all but a few thousand of the money his dad had left him via the sale of the family's home in Anaheim when he died, and was soon transformed into a frustrated, ill tempered, washed up cop with frequent domestic disturbances, and after deliberating for four months he made the decision to leave his wife. Before he could tell her about this, though, she left him and ran away with someone she had an ongoing affair with. A guy in the construction business. Grey was just about to leave his wife and had not done it because of the kids and because he felt sorry for her and he felt that he was all she had or could ever get, so her actually leaving him was a big shock to his system.

David was separated and waiting for his divorce to come through when he left the Los Angeles Police Department and started hanging out in Riverside. And he still had some of his inheritance left so in no time he started an Internet business. The business opened shop in downtown Riverside and eventually became quite well known. By that time Grey, whom everyone thought was just a cop, and whose name was on corporate filings and letterheads only, had started thinking about himself as a businessman. It was his business and he found out that he enjoyed the power of being the boss. But he was no marketer, and he didn't have a very good eye for opportunity and his business failed. He was deeply depressed when the bubble burst and had to get rid of his offices.

But by that time there were other things on his mind. He had hooked up with a girl who had high hopes of making a career out of him and his business. She was aggressive, and Grey really never had a chance of not being seduced by her. He also thought he was in love. When this girl saw that the business was doomed, along with the economy, she became disgusted with Grey and figured that she would get what she was going to get front and center, and so she booked a couple of flights out to Palm Desert through Palm Springs Airport, where she grew up and had gone to Junior College. During these years of travel for Grey and his new lady, the first was spent bumming around the desert, Palm Desert, Palm Springs, and the last two in Riverside. Grey had two friends: Jason and myself. Jason was his golf buddy, and I was his business buddy.

The girl who had hooked him, her name was Becky, was putting on considerable weight and so her attitude towards Dave changed from carelessness and exploitation to being determined to force him into marriage. All the while Grey had been supporting his mother with as much money as he could afford. And I don't think Grey looked at another woman this whole time. He was pretty happy, except that just like everyone else in Riverside he wished that he was living in Orange County, and he discovered the Internet. He started a subscription website that would notify clients of high-speed auto chases whenever they would occur. And they did occur often and people were always glued to the T.V. when they happened. Anywhere you were, if there was a high-speed chase going on, he would notify you by pager, text message, or email. It wasn't as bad a company as all his professional friends thought, but really the business model was not sound. He went to the gym, played golf, ran at the track, and went to the shooting range, and frequented many of the bars and restaurants in Riverside.

THE 909

I first found out about Becky's change in perspective one night after we all went out. We went to Mario's and afterwards went to a place called Back To The Grind for coffee. We had lattes and espressos and I said that I had to take off. Grey had been talking about the two of us going on a road trip. He wanted to get out of town and check out some nightlife. I thought it'd be a good idea to drive up to San Francisco and explore the coastline and more of the Mission district, or to hang around somewhere else south of Market. "I know a girl up in San Francisco that can show us around," I suggested.

Immediately I got a bad look from Becky. I thought it might be her dislike of her espresso drink, so I finished my sentence. "She's been up there since she graduated from Cal Poly. She's a great girl and will show us around in style."

She coughed and raised her eyebrows at me and was all uncomfortable looking and looked like she was getting bitchy. I'm not very good at reading these subliminal signals that women send, so the fact that I was picking up on her discontent meant that she was really not very happy about what I was suggesting.

"Actually," I said, "San Francisco is pretty far away for the weekend if we're driving. Let's drive out ot L.A." Los Angeles is a one-hour drive from Riverside.

Grey let out a big breath. Becky put a smile back on her face. I told them both that I hoped to see them soon and took off. Grey said he'd walk me to my car. "Jesus Christ," he said, "Why did you mention that girl in San Francisco? Did you see the look on Becky's face?"

"No. What are you talking about? If I know a girl up in the city what's it to Becky?"

"If there are any girls there – I can't go – period. Becky would never let it happen."
"You have got to be kidding me."
"Seriously. Becky would go bananas."
"O.K. Let's go to L.A. then"
"You're not mad about San Francisco?"
"L.A.'s a great city. We can go to L'Hermitage and Roscoe's or the House of Pies or The Dresden afterwards."
"That will be great."
"See you tomorrow for lunch," I said.
"Drive safe," he said, and went back inside The Grind.
"You forgot your sunglasses." He had left them on the hood of my car.
"Sorry." He walked back over to my car. "Sure you're all right about San Francisco?"
"Don't sweat it."
"See you tomorrow at lunch," he said. He walked back into the coffeehouse with his sunglasses and short haircut. He really was a nice enough guy. But that girl had him totally and utterly pussy whipped

CHAPTER TWO

That winter David got a tiny bit of investment capital for his website, and his subscriber base started to grow. He got some publicity on CNN – there were lots of high-speed auto chases these days and a company that tracked them was a good bit of news – real news being an increasingly scarce commodity. His good luck caused a big fight with Becky, I heard, and I think that's when she lost the war, because he also got lucky with some girls out in Newport Beach, and when he was back in Riverside he was a new man. He was more excited about the good life in Orange County than ever, and he was not the awkward cop anymore, and he wasn't such a nice guy anymore either. The media had loved his website and he got a big head about it. Girls were calling him on his cell phone, and his whole outlook on life had changed. For so many years he had been limited to his wife and as far as girlfriends, he had never seen anything beyond Becky. I'm sure he had never had and really good sex, though. And I'm sure he had never actually been in love.

You see, he married his first wife immediately after his terrible experience in high school. And then Becky had scooped him up right after his marriage fell apart. This was the first time that he had actually enjoyed being single. It was the first time in his life that hanging out with girls wasn't an accident or simply some sort of divine miracle. This changed David so that it just wasn't very much fun to hang out with him. He was brash and abrasive. At lunch he would brag about his conquests over and over, and I think he made some up, too. These couple of girls made him a bit too cocky for his own good. He liked bragging that one could always pick up a girl any night of the week if he wanted to just by going out to the right places.

There was something else. He had been reading too much of Men's Health, Maxim, GQ, and FHM magazines. This seems like a pretty innocent thing to do, but these magazines are bad for a guy without proper perspective. If you're not familiar with these magazines, let me explain. These magazines are full of pictures of strapping, tan, and well-dressed kids, luxury apartments and stainless steel gizmos that if you take too seriously at 26-years-old might drive you insane. These magazines suggest the life of a young millionaire – sports cars and yachts -- a perfect materialistic world created in print and existing nowhere. For a guy at 26 to think, "this is how I should live," is about as safe for his small fortune as an unlocked car in south central Los Angeles. Grey read every page of these magazines and took them all seriously. They were all it took for him to get the itch bad. I didn't realize how seriously he started to take them until one day he showed up in my office.

THE 909

"Hey Dave," I said. "How are things?"
"Would you like to be a partner with me in a yacht down in Newport?" he asked.
"No."
"Why not?"
"I don't know. Never wanted a partner in a boat. If I buy one I want to own it and sail it around the Islands. Also, it's too expensive. You can charter a yacht just the same."
"It's not like owning one."
"The girls don't know the difference."

I had client issues stacking up and needed the morning to finish some status reports. I liked to have everything done by one o'clock.
"What's one hundred fifty five times one oh eight?" I asked.
"Dunno."
"The high speed chase business slowing you down?"
"No; listen, Jack. If I took on three quarters of the expenses, would you go in as partner with me?"
"Why me?"
"You know boats. You've taken the Coast Guard classes. Your dad had a sailboat. You know lots of girls, too."
"No," I said. "I live Riverside and I go to Palm Desert in the summertime."
"All my life I've wanted to have a boat! I'll be too old to get any girls if I don't get a boat right now. Today."
"Don't even joke about that." I said. " You can get a boat anytime you want. You've got plenty of cash for the payments."
"I know, but I just can't take the plunge."
"Cheer up," I said. "The day you buy a boat is the day you want to sell a boat." My dad had told me this about his boat.

"I can't stand to think that I've got my youth now and it's slipping by. We'll all be thirty in no time. We've got to live it up while we can. Before we're all married with kids."
"Nobody really lives it up except rock stars. Who's in any hurry to get married anyhow?"
"I'm not interested in rock stars. They're the exception. I want to own a yacht with you down in Newport. We could have the time of our lives."
"Did you ever think about getting a sailboat and going down to Hawaii?"
"No I wouldn't like that."
"I'd go in on a sailboat with you."
"No; that doesn't interest me."
"That's because you didn't read about Hawaii in this month's GQ." Go on and check out some stories about single-handing around the world. That's where it's at."
"I want a yacht down in Newport."
      He had the broken-record-stubborn-cop bit down pat. I think they get training on that at the police academy.
"Let's go down to Lake Alice and have a beer."
"Don't you have any work to do?"
"No," I said.
      We went to Lake Alice, which was just downstairs. I had figured out the best way to get rid of friends I didn't want hanging around for too long. Once I was finished with my beer I would say I had to get back to work, go back up stairs, and they would have to offer to leave at that point. It was an important discovery, being a businessman and needing to keep up the appearance that my employees did all of my work for me. I had to keep up the image of a life of leisure, and that I didn't really do anything for the money I make. So we went down to Lake Alice and had a

couple of beers and a coffee. Grey checked the place out a little. "I like this place."
"Lot of booze to be had," I said.
"Check this out." he tipped his barstool forward.
"Do you realize that you'll be thirty in a couple of years and that you'll be doomed to being old, and never getting girls and never looking good or having fun anymore?"
"Sometimes, I guess."
"And that in a couple of years it'll be all over?"
"What?"
"I'm serious."
"I never worry about that kind of thing. For us men, things just get better with age. More power, and some of us even get better looking."
"You should live it up while you can, man."
"I got over that a long time ago. It's all a bunch of crap."
"Well, I want a yacht down in Newport."
"Listen, Dave, having flashy things doesn't get rid of your problems. You can't make your life better by filling it with material crap. It's all bullshit. Find out what you really need."
"But you've never had a yacht."
"If you had a fifty foot Tiera on Balboa, you'd feel exactly the same way then as you do now. Riverside is a good place to hang out. This is a great place. Why not start living in the present, here in Riverside."
"I'm sick of Riverside. I'm sick of downtown."
"Stay away from the downtown. Hang around in San Bernardino. See what kind of trouble you get into."
"I never find any kind of trouble. The only trouble I get into is when I get stopped by Riverside PD and have to flash my reserve badge."
"Downtown is a great place at night."

"I hate it here."
"Hey, listen, I've got to go check my email."
"Can't you check it later?"
"I'm expecting some important notes to come in today."
"Do you mind if I tag along with you?"
"Not at all."

He sat outside my office in the big couch by the receptionist and read some trade magazines like Computerworld and SAP Professional Journal. I worked with my assistant (they don't call them secretaries any more) for several hours to put together my invoices. She printed out all of the envelopes, address labels and calculated postage. Then I sent her to the post office to get the mail out before the pickup at 1:20pm. I went outside of my office, and there was Dave Grey asleep on the reception couch. He was asleep with his head on the armrest. I didn't want to wake him up, but I wanted to lock up and take off. So I put my hands on both his shoulders. He shook his head and said, "I didn't kill her. I didn't killer her."
"Dave," I said, and shook him again. He looked up. He wiped his eyes and woke up."
"Did I say anything just then?"
"You just mumbled. I couldn't understand anything."
"Man, what a nightmare!"
"Did the music put you to sleep?"
"I guess it did. Didn't sleep last night."
"What were you doing?"
"Arguing with Rebecca"

I could just see something like that keeping him up all night. One of my rare abilities is to put myself in the other guys' shoes. That, and picturing my friends' girlfriends naked, and what they'd look like in various centerfold arrangements. We went down to Lake Alice for

THE 909

a couple more rounds of beer. It was dead there so we went over to the blues bar next door and we each bought a cigar, which we lighted and smoked on our way over to the Presidential Lounge. There was a nice crowd, but it seemed like David had something on his mind and he said goodbye to me and so I went back over to Lake Alice.

CHAPTER THREE

It was one of those spring nights in Riverside when you can't wear anything more than a light shirt, shorts, and flip-flops. I sat at a table outside on the patio of Lake Alice after David had taken off, watching the sun go down, and the street lights come on, and a helicopter flew by loudly. The traffic signal to the left was blinking, and the horse carriage was going to the Mission Inn and Mario's place around the corner. I saw a nice pair of legs in a jeans skirt walk past the patio, on her way to the blues bar next door, lost sight of her and saw another coming up the street in the black hot-pants that you see so many girls wearing these days. Then, the first girl came back towards Lake Alice and we made eye contact and she came in and around to the patio and sat at the next table. I was chatting with the waitress at that time.
"Can I get you something?"
"Cozmo please."

"Watching too much sex in the city lately, are we?"
"Screw off ... Cozmo extra cranberry."
"I'll have one too, please," I said.
"What's up?" she asked. "Going out tonight?"
"Of course. Are you?"
"I don't know. There's nothing to do in this town."
"Don't you like Riverside?"
"No."
"Why don't you move to The OC?"
"I can't afford to live in Orange County," she said incredulously.
"And you can afford to live in Riverside?"
"I live with my parents."

  A cosmopolitan is served in a martini glass and is vodka, orange liqueur, and a bit of cranberry juice to make the drink red. It's supposed to be very popular and sophisticated to drink these kinds of drinks out of martini glasses. We sat and drank our cosmopolitans. The girl looked depressed.
"Well are we going to Mario's or Art's?" I didn't know her from Adam but the aggressive approach always works for me.

  She finally smiled and I could see why she had made a point of not laughing at my jokes. You might say that orthodontics never caught on in her family. Train wreck. I paid for the cosmos and we walked over across the way to the small parking lot where my car was. I would park it over behind Art's. We drove past the Mission Inn on our left, and the circular drive was packed with cars, their passengers waiting impatiently for the understaffed valet stand.
"Wasn't this a real mission once?" she asked me.
"Like with Indians and such?"

"Don't make fun of me."
"It used to be, but some guy bought it off the Indians for a quart of whiskey and some trinkets and turned it into a hotel. Never underestimate the power of capitalism."
"You're messing with me."

We turned right, past the Chinese gardens on our left, and the Riverside Brewing Company behind us, and turned into Art's lot. I parked the car and walked around to open the door for her. As she got out I put my arm around her trim waist and she pulled herself into me and tried to kiss me. She touched me with her other hand and I said, "whoa...."
"Sorry about that."
"What's wrong? Is there something the matter?"
"No."
"Then what's wrong?"
"No, nothing. It's O.K. It's O.K. Let's go." We walked out of the parking garage and over to Art's.
"You shouldn't leave me hanging like that if nothing is the matter."
"You shouldn't either. Well who cares? What's your problem?"
"What's your name?"
"Jennifer. What's yours?"
"Jack."
"Is that your Christian name?"
"I'm Catholic."
"It's a Christian name, too."
"No, I'm Catholic."
"Good, I hate Christians."

By this time we made it over to the entrance and she didn't like the look of the place at all. "Where are you taking me?" She grinned with all of her bad teeth.

THE 909

"This is Art's," I said. "If you'd rather go somewhere else, then go ahead. I'm eating here."
"Well the food must be good here because it's crowded."
"Better than most places."
We ordered some shrimp and a couple of steaks. We were just finishing up out first round of beer when the food came.
"This place isn't half bad," she said, "and the food is good."
"Better than the food on Main Street."
"University you mean."
"Uh, yeah."

We had a couple more beers each and Jennifer started to crack jokes. She showed me her pearly whites and I toasted to them.
"Cheers. Here's to your smile, beautiful."
"So what happened earlier," she said, "we should hang out some time."
"I've got a social disease," I said.
"You mean you're seeing a shrink?"
"Yeah."

We went on to talk about psychotherapy and she insisted that it was all just a bunch of mumbo-jumbo, and that people can't heal themselves and that mental illness was just a bunch of malarkey. I don't think she ever knew anyone with a serious mental disorder. All of a sudden the door burst open and someone yelled, "BAKER!"
"They recognized my car," I told her and went to greet them outside.
There was Jason, Grey, Jessica, and several other people that I did not know.

"You're coming to the Fox with us, aren't you Jack? We're all headed over there now," Jessica said from the passenger window.
"Jack, get in your car. Let's go." Jason said. "Let's go man!"
"All right all right, I'm eating dinner here."
"Who are you here with?" Jessica called out from the car smiling. She was Jason's girlfriend and knew me pretty well.
"We'll be there in a few," I said ignoring her question. And went back in.
"Where are your friends going?" Jennifer asked.
"They're headed over to the Red Fox in San Bernardino."
"What do they do?"
"They work in retail."
"Lots of people these days in retail."
"Yup."
"They make good money, though."
"Definitely."
    We finished up our steaks and beers. "Let's go," I said.
"We're going to have some tequila and Corona's with my friends."
    Jennifer fished some makeup things out of her bag and painted on more makeup while I paid the tab. And apart from her teeth, she really did look pretty good.
"Let's go," she said.
    We got right on the 215 from Art's and headed up to the Red Fox in San Bernardino. We parked the car in the dirt lot right behind the place where my buddy's car hard been broken into and wandered over to the entrance.
"Hey this is the girl that I've been living with, Jennifer Loebe."

"Oh my god! Are you related to Lisa Loebe the singer?" Jessica said, "You look just like her!"

"Not at all. My name is Jennifer Koenig." She really was that good looking, I guess.

"He's fucking with me." Jennifer said.

"Hey did you hear that," Jessica said, "He's dating Lisa Loebe!" He introduces us to her without even telling us that she's a big rock star and all!"

"No, my name is..."

"LISA LOEBE!" Marcus chimes in.

"Of course, Jennifer Koenig. We go way back," Jessica smiles and hugs her and is always charming with other women. It's a skill she has deployed on my behalf with other women several times.

"Who is she?" Jessica asks me in my ear. "Do I have to be nice to her?"

She turns to Jennifer with a fake smile. She crosses her legs in a mock proper posture and begins a formal conversation.

"No, I hate Riverside. There's nothing to do out here."

"Really, I love it here. There's so much to do."

"I think it's boring."

"How interesting. Maybe you haven't been here very long?"

"I've lived here all my life."

"But the people are wonderful, you have to admit." Jennifer whispers into my ear, "I love your friends."

Jessica was drunk and would loved to continue harassing my date, but some of the people were getting up to sing at the Karaoke stage.

Diane was the "KJ" and she dished out instrumental versions of the classics for drunken karaoke singers six nights a week. The Red Fox was open every day. Diane had

taken to using a pair of crutches due to a recent knee surgery. There were cleverly placed mirrors that made the Red Fox look larger than it was, and the mirrors separated the billiards room from the bar. Diane came in on her crutches closer to the bar as we were moving towards the stage and the dance floor. There were several standing tables with stools right near the stage and we moved to those. "I wish they had better songs in these Karaoke books," Jason said. Diane came up and wanted to know what the girls would sing. Jessica and Nichole got up on stage and sang, "I Will Survive." We all went out on the dance floor and danced and sang to the lyrics. We came off the dance floor all sweaty.
"Damn this place gets hot!" Jennifer said.
"It's pretty damn hot, yes."
"Jesus it's hot!"
"Take off your shirt." I wondered if she was drunk enough to fall for it.
"That's a good idea." She was.

Marcus grabbed Jennifer and started dancing with her and her black bra. I went back over to the bar. It was steaming in the bar and it was nice with the music and cold beer. I wandered over to the door. A couple of black Mercedes with gold trim and deep-dish rims pulled into the parking lot next to my car. A crowd of really large, dark men with long hair, some in hockey team shirts, others in t-shirts walked up. They were all covered with tattoos. Sleeves. The bouncer standing at the door looked over to me with his eyebrows raised. They all piled into the bar. As they came into the light I saw their dark red skin, sharp cheekbones, long black hair, grinning, talking their native Wind-talker language. One of them saw Jennifer with just her bra on and said, "There's a good one for you."

The largest one – he really was a mountainous one and I think his name was Tiny said, "Go on."
The first one grunted and lumbered out to the dance floor. Kelley was with them.
I was fuming angry. They always pissed me off. I know we took their land and that it was all a joke that they have this casino money, but it still pissed me off nonetheless. They had to shove it in your face. And I wanted to crack one of them up. Kick one of their rears and break their stuck-up I've-got-more-money-than-god bullshit. I went outside to have a smoke. The smoke made me sick to my stomach and the last of my beer was warm, which made matters worse. When I came back in there they had monopolized the dance floor and Jennifer was dancing with the huge one, who was barely moving. Kind of rocking back and forth. He was sort of holding her waist and looked like he was trying to hump her on the dance floor. Another song was being sung to now and another one of them asked her to dance. She was one of theirs now. They do this shit every time.
I went back to one of the red plastic booths back by the bar and sat down. Grey was there. Becky was dancing. Jessica brought a huge one over. "This is Billy Lightfoot." He was from the Pechanga tribe, living in Colton. I asked him to have a beer with us.
"Got my own beer."
"Can I get you another?"
"O.K."
We got Joel the bartender to bring us a couple more Heinekens.
"You own a company in town they tell me."
"Yeah."
"Do you like it in Riverside?"

"Yes."
"Really?"
You could say that I was drunk at this point. Not totally messed up, but drunk enough to say what I meant.
"Of course I like it," I said, "yes. Don't you like it here?"
"Jeez."
  I took off and went back to the dance floor. Jessica followed me over there. "Don't get mad at Billy."
"I wasn't mad, I was just about to puke my guts out."
"Your new live-in is having a good time," Jessica pointed out.
"She is," I said.
"Check her out," said Jessica.
  Grey came over "Let's do those shots," he said, "Anejo."
  We went back over to the bar.
"What's up, man?"
"It's nothing. These guys make me sick."
  Kelley came up to us.
"Hey guys."
"Hey Kelley," I said. "You're pretty drunk tonight?"
"I'm never going to drink again. I'll have another shot, please. Anejo?"
  She stood about to take the shot and I saw Grey looking at her. He gave her a long, hard look. He looked her up and down again.
  Kelley was a very good-looking girl. She wore a sleeveless white knit top and a denim skirt with the rear end faded and well above her knees that left exactly what you wanted left to your imagination and no more. She had sun streaked sandy brown hair and tanned legs to match. She was a thoroughbred, and you could tell she knew how to use her body.

The 909

"Did you come in with those guys?" I asked.

"They are so much fun. And so nice. Give them a chance, would you? When did you get here?"

"Couple minutes ago."

"Are you having a good time?"

"Wonderful."

"Come on, now. Look at Jessica and Nichole and the other girls. Go out and have a good time."

She was trying to get Grey to go over to the dance floor.

"Drinking less these days are we? Cutting back a bit?" I said.

"Definitely, I have to watch myself with the guys I came in with."

Another popular tune started in and David Grey said, "Let's dance, Kelley."

Kelley smiled and sighed, "This is Jack's and my song." She was laughing. "What kind of a name is Jack anyhow? Is that Christian?"

"How about the next song?" Grey interrupted.

"Jack and I are taking off after this," Kelley said. "We're heading back downtown."

When we moved over to the dance floor and started to dance a little I could tell Dave was still checking her out. He couldn't take his eyes off of her ass. To tell you the truth, you could hardly blame him.

"You've got a new member for your fan club, there" I said to her.

"Come on now. That poor guy. I didn't even notice him until he asked me to dance at the bar."

"Girls all love a little attention."

"Not from that kind of guy."

"Yes, even from that kind of guy."

"Well, what if I do like the attention?"
"Nothing," I said.

I was spinning her around on the dance floor to some obscure song, mocking the drunks who were seriously pathetic looking. I pulled her in close and she felt skinny and soft in all of the right places against me. We passed Jennifer, shirt back on, dancing with one of the band of Indians. I mean Native Americans.
"Why on earth did you bring her here?"
"Maybe for one of the guys. Do a threesome later."
"You're such a nice guy."
"I just need to keep busy is all."
"Are you busy now?"
"Doing fine just now."
"Let's go to your place."
"You want to?"
"I wouldn't mention it if I didn't want to go, Jack."

We walked back to the bar from the dance floor and I got my leather jacket from our first table while Kelley stood by the bar. Grey was on her. I asked Joel at the bar to watch for Jennifer and if she asked where I was to put her tab on mine. Otherwise, if she left with the guys she was with, just to put her on their tab. I gave him a twenty.
"Leaving this early?"
"Take care, Joel."

I went back to the front of the bar and Grey was still hitting on Kelley. She told Dave she would talk to him later and she grabbed my rear end.
"You're going to make your new girlfriend mad," Kelley said.
"Oh, yeah."
"You're O.K. to drive?"
"Always."

"Sure you don't want to stop downtown for another?"
"That's all right."
"Well at least we've escaped that crowd."

We stood against the passenger side door of my car out in the lot and didn't say anything but we were looking into each other's eyes. Finally, I opened the door for her and went around the back of the car and got in and started the car.

"I've never been so goddamn depressed, Jack." Kelley said.

CHAPTER FOUR

I drove back down the 215 onto the 60, passed the University, and then swerved right up the dark stretch of freeway, got off at Central, down a hill and then back on level ground down to Canyon Crest behind Ralph's. The only thing open was the doughnut shop, and only through a little window at that time of night. Even the Denny's, open 24-hours a day anywhere else, closes at 1:00AM in Riverside. I went around to open the door for Kelley but she was already out of the car coming closer to me. I went over to her and held her hand. We decided to walk over and see if anyone was over at the cafe even though we both knew it was deserted. The shape of her body and the smell of her hair haunted me. The brush of her hips was against my side. I could see her face under the sodium light of the parking lot lights. We made it over by the Japanese food place and Papis and it was darker there, so I pulled her around to face me and I kissed her and felt her waist and

THE 909

pulled her into me and she pulled me into her very firmly and finally she pushed me away. Her eyes were on fire.
"Don't ever do that again."
"What?"
"I can't go through this again."
"Come on Kelley."
"Don't do this. We can't. You understand. I can't do it, period. Jack, you understand don't you? Don't you?"
"I thought we were in love?"
"Of course, you know I melt away to nothing in your arms."
"You know there are things we can do about this."

She was holding my hand again now and brushing herself up against me again and we continued our walk through the deserted parking lot under the sodium lights. We had both calmed ourselves down a bit. She kept looking at me with those eyes. That face. Those pale blue eyes that you never fully believed could actually exist on a human and provide good sight for their owner. She looked at me like she would be mine and would follow me to the end of the earth, but I knew she couldn't go nearly that far with me.
"There's no cure."
"You know about that stuff, you're on them. It's safer. I just can't do it."
"We need to *not* see each other."
"But we have to."
"It's me. Of course it's my fault, my burden. What comes around goes around, you know. You get what you deserve." She had been staring at me with those unreal eyes the whole time and you could tell she was zoning out. They snapped back into focus.

"I've done my share to the men in my life, you know that. What comes around goes around for me too."
"Forget about all that," I said. "This was never supposed to happen to me. I still don't believe it's real. It can't be real."
"Don't even go there."
"Let's just forget about it for now, can't we?"
"I sort of wonder about it sometimes, if I could have gotten it too, but nobody ever thinks that it'll happen to them."
"No," I said. "They don't."

It was such a great romantic topic to talk about. Guaranteed to win the ladies over instantly. Of course I had considered just keeping it in the dark with girls, but that is just not an option.
"It's so great, you know, being in love with you. Better than I expected it would be."
"It really is," she said, she was zoning again.
"I don't mean great as in swell or good or anything just that it's not boring or anything."
"Bull. It sucks."
"I'm glad we saw each other tonight."
"I don't think we should see each other any more, ever."
"I need it. Please don't go."

We were standing now by the Rite Aid with the Bank of America and the Carl's Junior in view, all empty, all dead. We were completely alone and she was an absolute stranger to me now. She had an uncanny way of turning it all off -- just like that.
"Where should we go now?" I asked. She looked back to the car.
"Let's go to Mario's."

We drove right over to Mario's taking side streets. We wound down Central and up Chicago. Past the Mexican place that's always jumping, the post office, and the low

The 909

budget grocer on the right. Then up University through the barrio and finally under the train tracks to downtown and past Art's and RBC. We were quiet the whole way there. She finally said something, "Can you do me a favor?"
"Sure."
"Kiss me."

We finally got out of the car at the valet stand at the Mission Inn. The valet opened the door for Kelley and I stepped out of the car putting on my jacket and taking the ticket from the guy. "I look like crap." She pulled her hair back into a ponytail and wrapped a black velvet band around it several times. We found most of the regulars plus our friends across the street in Mario's at the bar.
"Hey you guys," Kelley said. "I'm going to have another shot."
"Hey Kelley, how's it going!" Dwight the businessman, whom everyone called "Dog", came up behind her. "Drinking tequila tonight?"
"Hey Dog," Kelley said."
"This is my friend, Chris," Dog said. A good-looking, and obviously cocky guy came over and admired her curves.
"Riverside is *absolutely fabulous* these days," Chris said.
"Oh yeah…" Kelley said, "The 909 rocks."
Jason called me over to his part of the bar, "Mr. Jack Baker," he said, "You'd better take this shot. That chick you brought is fucked up and she's pretty drama."
"What happened?"
"She went home with one of the Indians. She's fucking white trash man. Excellent vocabulary. Let's have another Corona."
"I'm driving. Hey, have you seen Grey?"
"He left with Becky," Jessica added.
"I told you that guy's whipped!"

Someone made a whip cracking sound.

"Oh yeah," said Jessica.

"I'm out," I said. "You guys drive safe."

I told Kelley I was leaving and said goodbye to her at the bar. Chris was buying a round of shots. "Take this one, Jack!"

"Seriously, guys, I'm driving."

"You're really taking off now?" Kelley asked me.

"Yeah," I said. "I've got one of those migraines."

"See you tomorrow?"

"Come see me in the office."

"Yeah right."

"All right, where, then?"

"Anywhere after I get home from work."

"Let's do it at seven."

"O.K. let's meet at Duane's."

"See you there."

"Heard from Jon?"

"Got an email today."

"Later Jack," Chris said.

I left Mario's and out across the street to The Mission Inn, with the infinity of white twinkle lights up year-round now, instead of just at Christmas. I gave my ticket to the valet along with a twenty and took a peek inside. The bar and Duane's were winding down. Someone inside Duane's waved at me. I think it was one of my Computer Science professors from the University. I wanted to get to sleep, so I went back to get my car. I passed by Sangria, The Spaghetti Factory, and then into the deep barrio of Riverside. My place was across town in the Canyon Crest Villas but I liked to take the long route home. I drove past a crack house that I had been to one time. I went with my stripper friends who lived next door. They needed a man around to be present during a large weed purchase. The purchase was to the tune of about a thousand or so dollars. Very large. Very big deal. They wanted someone with negotiating skills, and they insisted that I go.

I pulled into my garage, wondering if my stripper friends down the way were back home yet. They all lived together and worked at the Spearmint Rhino in Rancho Cucamonga, and never got home before three in the morning. And then they would invite me to come over and smoke weed and drink beer with them as they wound down for the evening. But they weren't home so I pulled out my keys and went over to my mailbox. There was the assorted junk mail, plus a card and some bank statements. The card was from a long lost high school date that had called my parent's house to get my new address. She was now the proud mother of about five kids from as many fathers and wanted to know what I was up to. Did she want another one?

Well anyway she had fond memories of the days past and was probably wondering if I turned out to be as decent as I was when I was a kid. I'm not so sure about that one, kiddo, not so sure at all. Anyhow forget about all of that and forget her, too.

I finally made it upstairs to my bedroom, turned on the lights and made one last final check of my email and opened up the window across the way. My bed was up against the opposite wall and I took off my clothes, throwing them over the back of my desk chair. I could hear some cars driving by on El Cerrito, one with the booming, popping exhaust of a tricked out Acura. We call them "homey vehicles." Cars could keep you awake when you had a hard time sleeping around here. I had a sort of full-length mirror leaning up against the same wall as my window and I looked at my face. Was this the sort of face that took the shape of an early death? I was handsome now and had all of my hair. I couldn't imagine what I'd look like dead and shuddered at the thought, and I knew I would go that way and I just hoped it would be quick. That wasn't often the case. How the hell did it come to me? What a joke. I had some pajama bottoms that I liked to wear. Just the pants. So I stepped into these and climbed into bed with a couple of magazines. I grabbed copies of *The OC Weekly* and *Motorcycle Magazine*. Commie Girl was my favorite columnist with her sarcastic and brilliant wit. I think I'd like her if I ever met her. I read the OC Weekly cover to cover, including all of those escort and stripper classifieds that they seem to have more and more of these days.

Then I couldn't read any more about motorcycles and I couldn't ready anything more about music or the art scene in Orange Country and I started to think about my situation. I grew up hearing about this kind of thing. Everyone talked about it. Better be careful. Right. Was anyone? No. All the educated types know that it was impossible. No, not virtually impossible, scientifically impossible. What about Magic Johnson? I laughed out loud to the thought of that, "That guy had a lot of bitches," My friend Dwight had told me.

I guess I was in denial for some time. And when people would lower their eyes and shake their heads, and maybe even see me coming down the street and cross over to the other side, it was O.K. People, especially here don't like to share grief – they'd rather leave you alone. They don't want to intrude. I understood. I'd act the same way, maybe. And things were going along well until I saw Kelley in Riverside again after I had to leave my place in

Manhattan Beach. She always likes a challenge. Always has. And just try and forget about that, Jack Baker. Try to forget about her. Try to forget about how beautiful she is. Yeah, right.

I had my eyes closed but I wasn't sleepy and my mind started to wander to my business, my family, and then always back to Kelley. And then the business and the other practicalities of life faded into the background and I started think more about Kelley and how well put together her body was, but not in an erotic way. And this thought came in and out of my mind in waves growing more intense and more intense. In a way that made me think about my situation and I sort of started to cry. And when it was done I felt better and went to sleep.

My eyes always shoot right open and I look all around in different directions like bug eyes when I'm woken up out of a deep sleep. Someone was downstairs and someone was being really loud, and banging on my door and ringing my doorbell. My heart was pounding.
"Hey open up! Are you there?"
"Yeah."

Vanessa, my next-door neighbor was calling up to me.
"There's a drunk chick down here we opened the gate for and you'd better come get her before she pukes on my rugs." They had red carpet with zebra rugs all around their apartment and a huge big screen television that never worked.

Then I heard Kelley's slurring. In my daze I thought that it could have been Jennifer.
"Sorry Jack," she said. "Did I wake your friends up?" She was completely hammered. "Don't get pissed. Were you saleeping?"

"What do you think?"

Looking over at the clock it looked like almost five in the morning.

"Oh my god, I had no idea what time it was," Kelley said. She sat down on my bed with me. "Chris brought me here."

"Um, yah. So what's he like?" I was just coming back upstairs from the kitchen with some bottles of water for the both of us.

"Thank you," she said. "Chris? He's a really nice guy. We're what you would call socially compatible."

"Is he a drug dealer?"

"Could be. You know he probably is. Where he gets all of that cash, I'll never know. And his phone is always ringing and he's always answering in quick cryptic sentences."

She drinks half of her water in one pull from the bottle.

"I think maybe he's selling weed. Pretty big time – but he's cool for sure. I can tell."

"Are you going to keep hanging out with him?"

"Oh, no, I couldn't do that."

"Huh?"

"You know he offered me two thousand dollars if I would go to San Diego with him this weekend. Told him I couldn't do it. I told him that I knew too many people in San Diego. He asked if he could take me to L.A., and I told him I know too many people in L.A., it's true! He was really nice about it, though."

"What do you think about all of this? You know Kevin's a good guy, don't you?"

"Is Kevin really loaded too?"

Kevin was another one of Kelley's regular "friends." I'm sure they have had an ongoing affair for the past several years, and maybe even during the time that Kelley and I were together. That being said, Kevin was one of Kelley's friends that I actually did like.

"No doubt about it. Where have you gone with him again?"

"New York, Costa Rica, Vancouver, Hong Kong, Hawaii, Park City."

"Drink your water."

"Don't look at me like that," she said. "I told him that I'm in love with you and that I always will have feelings for you, no matter what happens. He was nice about that, too. He wants us all to go to dinner this weekend. Want to come?"

"Sure. What about Jason or David?"

"Shit, I've got to get out of here."

"Why?"

"I just wanted to see you, that's all. How stupid of me. Didn't' I tell you? Chris dropped me off here, and I told Kevin to come pick me up. I think Kevin's outside in his car waiting for me."

"Kevin Manning?"

"Uh, yeah. We're going to head over to IHOP and have breakfast. He just flew in to LAX tonight. Want to come with us for some pancakes?"

"He's here? Shit. Hey, I'm way too tired to be any fun."

"Come on."

"No. Tell him I said hi."

"O.K."

"Good night baby."

"Don't get all mushy on me."

I kissed her lips and she shivered. "I'd better get out of here," she said. "Good night Jack."

"You know you can stay here."

"Yeah I know."

We made out a little bit more on her way down to the front door. She was going down the stairs before me and I couldn't resist the shape of her body lying down on the stairs and me on top of her so I pulled her down onto the steps and finally I let her out of the front door.

I went up stairs quickly so that I could watch her get into Kevin's silver 911 convertible and drive away down Chicago to the IHOP on University. Of course I thought of her having breakfast with Kevin and then going back to his place. And this was the girl I was crying over just a couple of minutes ago. Except that he lives in San Francisco so that his place will be a hotel – and Kelley and Kevin checking into a hotel room gets me to feeling like shit again.

CHAPTER FIVE

The next morning I stumbled out of bed and walked across the parking lot to the cafe for a bagel and a latte. It was one of those great desert mornings. It had rained enough that winter and the grass was growing on Box Springs Canyon Mountain and the wind was cool and it was blowing from the east. It brought in the smell of grass and faint smell of fertilizer. I read the Los Angeles Times and the Wall Street Journal. University students were coming to the bus stop nearby heading the short way to campus. From the cafe I walked back over to my car and drove downtown via the 91 over and down Allesandro. I passed Madison and 14th street and parked in the covered lot around the corner from my office. It was rush hour and the freeway was packed with cars. Ahead of me I saw a bumper sticker that read 'world famous KROQ'. Everyone was going to work. I saw one guy shave with an electric razor and a lady was putting on her lipstick in her rear view mirror. It felt nice to be driving into work like a regular person.

Upstairs in my office my assistant was waiting with some phone messages and last week's mail. I read some of the online versions of the newspapers that I read over breakfast. At about 11:30 I sent off a bunch of over-due notices to clients that haven't paid last months bills yet. It's one of those days when my fingers don't follow my brain's orders. Maybe they're too cold for typing. But the typing is slow going with lots of errors. In reading the papers I learned that our president George Bush had some opinions about Saddam Hussein.

"He's dodged, craw-fished, and wheedled his way out of everything, …" Bush said.

I laugh when I recall that mudbug is another word for crawfish. And that a couple of years ago on a trip to New Orleans with my folks, in the French Quarter, the Cajun people would boil the miniature little red lobsters in Tabasco water. It was fun to pull their heads off, suck out the spicy juice and then peel and eat the rest of the meat out of their bodies with our fingers.

"Haven't seen you out in Newport," Orlando said.

"Oh, I've been hanging out in Riverside."

"I've got to stick around one night and see what you guys have going on out here. Maybe we should go t Margaritaville one night. That's a good place, isn't it?"

"Yes. That or this new dive bar we've been hanging out at. The Red Fox."

THE 909

"I've been meaning to get over there." Obviously he had never heard of the place. Well, you know how it is with a boyfriend and all. Tough to get out."
"I thought Riverside boys had their girls-nights-out."
"You would think," said Orlando. "I haven't been out forever. Well, someday I'll be single and then I'll have my fair share of going out again. That's the good life. Live single and buy a sports car."
"I've been thinking of picking up one of those little German jobs." We were on our way down to lunch.
"Coming into Lake Alice for a beer?"
"Thanks, man. I've got to get some work done today."
"See you later."
"Later." I gave him a little nod and walked back to the elevator. David Grey was waiting in the lobby upstairs.
"Hello Jack," he said. "Are you going out to lunch?"
"Yes."
"Where should we go?"
"I can eat anything."
 I was sitting behind my desk looking at him. "Where do you want to go?"
"How about RBC? They've got good appetizers."
 Inside the bar area we ordered appetizers and some beer. The sorority girl brought the dark, freezing cold, beer that they brewed there on-site. You could see all of the equipment, very much in use at every moment on your way into the bar. There were a dozen good beers, ales and stouts that you could order here. And also the fried foods and pub grub were brought out right after the beer. Someone behind the bar rang a bell and shouted the conspicuous chant because a kid from The O.C. ordered a bottle Bud or a Corona rather than a local beer.
"Anything interesting happen last night?" I asked Grey.

"Can't remember."
"How's business going?"
"Sucks. Can't seem to get my billing system squared away. My customers are always late in paying."
"That's pretty normal."
"I know it is."
"Thought any more about that yacht in Newport?"
"Hey I still can't live without a boat."
"Why don't you take the plunge?"
"It's Becky."
"Buy it anyway."
"She doesn't like boats. She's just not into the ocean. She doesn't even like the beach."
"Tell her to beat it, then."
"Are you kidding? I couldn't do that."
He finished off his second ale and leveled his beady eyes at me.
"Hey, what do you know about Kelley?"
"Her name is Kelley Taylor. Rich parents from Palm Desert. Very smart. She's a nice girl," I said. "She's getting a divorce and she's planning to marry Jon Bushnell. He lives up in San Francisco right now. Why?"
"She is the most incredible girl I have ever seen in my life."
"She is, isn't she?"
"There's just something about her. Her legs. Arms. How she moves."
"She's smart."
"I can't really describe it. Class. In the genes."
"Sounds like you're into her."
"She drinks like a fish," I said. "She's in love with Jon Bushnell and she's going to marry him. She's going to be filthy rich some day."
"She won't marry that guy."

"Oh, no?"
"No way. Never. How long have you known her?"
"Long time. Ten years. She was in my honors classes back at the University."
"She must have been young back then."
"She's 26 now. She's still hot, too."
"When did she marry Woods?"
"Right after college. Her true love ran away to be a part of some Internet startup company."
"You sound bitter about that."
"Oh, I don't mean to at all. Can't argue the facts, man."
"I still don't think she would marry someone just for his money."
"Well, she's already done it once."
"No way."
"Well," I said, "don't ask if you don't want to know."
"I didn't ask."
"You asked me what I know about Kelley."
"You didn't have to start talking shit."
"Go to hell, man."
He stood up with his bullshit cop presence and just stared at me, his face red and angry.
"You'd better apologize for that."
"Alright man. Calm down. Stay in Riverside."
"What?"
"Sit down. We're just getting started on this food here."
"You really need to watch what you say about people."
"Yeah, yeah. You're right. You really are. I can say some things I don't mean some times. You're right."
"I know," Grey said. "Jack you know you're my best friend."

With friends like this who needs friends.

"Sorry about the go to hell business," I said out loud this time.

"I'm sorry."

"It's cool man. It was just all that about Kelley."

"Alright. Let's eat."

We finished up the plate of fried things and some chicken. We walked back downtown and I just knew that Grey wanted to talk more about Kelley. I took off and came back up to the office.

CHAPTER SIX

At seven I was at the Mission Inn for a date with Kelley. She hadn't shown up so I was making some notes to myself on their stationery. I sat around for about an hour and then went to the bar at Duane's and had a gin martini, straight up with extra olives. Kelley wasn't in the bar and she wasn't in the restaurant. So I went over to the Red Fox in San Bernardino. It was always nice driving on the freeways with my CD player blasting. With the sunroof down letting in some of the desert heat, it was especially nice. I passed the Boot Barn sign, all broken and run down so now it just reads, "Bot Barn." Signs out here are in the habit of not getting fixed. Posters for the many local strip clubs, cowboy boots and clothing stores, and local slum neighborhoods of San Bernardino abut the freeway. Prime real estate, really. There's a Caterpillar tractor office building and other signs of its semi-rural status. Now I was driving through Grand Terrace and through Colton. You never notice when you drive through this city. There are the all the signs that you are out of the major suburbs. Things that make a place all right to live in, but terrible to just drive through if you're paying attention to the details. There are many other freeways that are just as ugly as the one that runs from Riverside to San Bernardino, but none that I hate more. Maybe this is how most people feel about all of The 909. I wonder where most people get their inability to love it out here. Probably from something they read. No, more likely something they heard or saw on T.V. So many people get their likes and dislikes from T.V. Or they get them from the radio. There are a couple of radio D.J.'s that have launched campaigns against this part of Southern California. I'm sure this is why most people don't like it out here. But like anywhere else in the world, there are good people here and it's always the people that make place.

    I stopped out in front of The Red Fox. There really wasn't any other place in San Bernardino. I'm sure that in ten years from now this will still be the only place around. There were some people inside the bar and a few outside smoking. You can smoke inside the bar, contrary to California state law, but there are mostly polite people out here. They're polite because lots of people have gun collections in the trunks of their cars. Guns in trunks tend to breed politeness in a community.

"Come over here man," Dwight said, "Where have you been?"
"What's going on?"
"Nothing."
"Been out to the desert?"
"No, not since last weekend."
"Any new hookups?"

"Nope."
"What's wrong?"
"I don't know. I'm sick of the whole scene. I'm done."
He tipped his chair forward and looked at me.
"Can I tell you something, Jack?"
"Sure."
"I haven't been laid for a week."

Dwight Jacobson was the most avid womanizer I had met to date and you could rely on a certain regularity in his sex schedule and of his hooking up with new women. It seemed just last week that he had called me up to tell me that he had just gotten lucky with a couple of girls in Vegas and could I come watch the whole video of it with him? Or was it that he had just gotten a blowjob while standing fully erect on a barstool?

"What's wrong?"
"I don't have any cash," he smiled, "I just can't seem to have any luck when I'm broke. Girls just won't even look at me."
"You're just looking in the wrong places, man. You know money is the last thing girls go for. We've talked about this before. It's nothing."

"I've got plenty of cash, let's go eat."

I put three one hundred dollar bills down to pay for our tab.

"You don't ever watch T.V. do you, man?"

"Mostly movies. I did check out that show called American Superstar. Some cute girls but that show is really stupid."

"What a surprise."
"It's over now. I think they're going to have the winner sing at the Lincoln Memorial on September 11th."
"What a surprise."

We sat there to think about how utterly stupid and asinine the thought of this was.

"I guess T.V. is alright, I just can't watch it."

"Another Corona?"

"Cool."

"Here comes Grey," I said. He was just coming in thru the door.

"That jackass. I hate that guy," Dwight said. Grey came up to us at the bar.

"Hello David, I was just telling Jack here what a jack ass you are." Dwight smiled.

"What?"

"OK, I have a question for you. If you had all the money in the world and you didn't need to work, what would you do?"

Grey just sat there and stared at Dwight.

"Don't think about it. Just tell us."

"I don't know. What are you talking about?"

"Seriously. If you had unlimited resources, what would you do? What comes to mind?"

"I don't know. I guess I would just get laid a lot."

"I was wrong, Grey. You're not a jackass, you're just stupid."

"Ha Ha. Very funny Dwight," Grey said. "Someday you're going to get shot."

Dwight Jacobson laughed in his face. "You think so? I don't think so because people actually *like* me. And if I get shot, who cares?"

"You'd care if you got shot."

"No it wouldn't. I don't give shit."

"Dwight, let's have another shot," I said.

"It's cool man, I'm going to get something to eat. Later, Jack."

He left the bar and pushed the swinging door open with confidence. That's what everybody likes about him.

"That guy always pisses me off," Grey said.

"I grew up with him. I like him. He's a good guy. You just need to joke around with him some more. Relax."

"I know. It just pisses me off. He never has any money."

"He's got enough. Get any work done this morning?"

"No. I just can't get started on anything. It's harder to sell subscriptions to websites these days. People don't want to pay for what they can get for free."

The arrogance that he had after his financing came through, and after he had gotten so lucky down in Newport with his new girls was finished. Actually, I don't think I noticed a big change in David until he fell in love with Kelley. Back then he was all too sure of himself and his ability to sell a million subscriptions to his high speed chase notification service. Back then he was absolutely sure of his own abilities and his need to spend and make more money. Back during all of that business with him talking about the yacht in Newport Beach and his confidence about girls. But somehow I don't think I've communicated clearly about David Grey. He was a pretty good-looking man. He had a good golf swing, he ran every day, and had kept himself in good shape since the police academy. Also his work on the police reserve kept him in the gym and working out and looking fit. He handled the weights in the gym well and was good with the exercises. He also played a good hand of bridge and knew how to roll the dice in Vegas. And he could hold his own with girls on a very superficial level. He was in the habit of wearing those old seventies style shirts that came back into fashion, and he had a good tan. He could wear clothes that were a bit young for the rest of us and pull it off. He had a certain quality of youthful

naiveté that would cause him to get offended easily because of a misunderstanding in any given situation. He was still a bit of a homebody and had been seriously involved with women who would take care of his every need for him. He also took great pride in being better than other people at different things. He hated to lose at golf and he hated when he went home alone any given night without a girl. When he fell in love with Kelley his concentration and intensity fell at the gym and guys that he would always out-lift started to catch up to him. He didn't seem mad about this at all.
We were sitting here at the bar in the Red Fox in Colton and Dwight Jacobson had just walked out of the door.
"Come with us over to the Barn."
"Sorry, I have a date tonight."
"When?"
"Becky is coming here at eight."
"Speaking of the devil."
Becky Vera came into the bar through the door, throwing it back quickly like it was an unwanted nuisance. She was a very well proportioned girl and all of her parts moved in concert when she walked. She had a great ass.
"Hi," she said in the characteristic high-pitched fake American way. "Oh, I'm glad you're here Jack. I've been wanting to talk to you."
"Hey Beck," Dave smiled.
"Hello there, David. I didn't see you there." She was ignoring him talking to me in her rapid-fire animated way,
"I've had the worst afternoon. Where were you David?"
"We didn't have plans did we?"
"I went to meet Kelley in Long Beach for lunch and I had to drive all the way out there and she wasn't there so I

THE 909

came back to meet up with David at The Mission Inn. But of course I can't afford to eat there because he took his credit card back. So I went to Mario's but you weren't there."

"What did you do?"

"I went shopping at Tyler." I got the impression that she was always fake like this to everyone. Maybe she even faked herself out most of the time.

"So how are you doing, Jack?"

"Fine."

"I just loved your date the other night, what was her name?" She didn't wait for a response, "she was so nice, and you took off so early. And with that Kelley girl."

"You don't like Kelley?"

"Oh she's very nice, and she's got a *nice ass* ... don't you think so, David?"

He kept his mouth shut.

"Jack I need to talk to you. Alone. Stay here David."

"What's going on Becky?"

"He's going to leave me. I just know he's going to leave me. He hasn't had sex with enough women yet so he's going to leave."

She looked at me and her eyes were glazing over with tears but the tears well up and fall out, they just stayed and covered her whole eyeball. I think she had gotten good at this. She had done this before.

"I wouldn't marry him anyhow. Even if he asked me to. He doesn't know how to treat a woman. And I've wasted the best years of my life on him. And just after I had gotten over that abortion I had before him."

I kept my mouth shut again.

"We had gotten through that rotten abortion together, and instead we just fought all the time. We had big, loud, violent fights. He tied me up once with zip ties, the kind that those dirty bastard cops use as handcuffs when there are too many people crossing the border. He tied me up with cheap handcuffs like a rotten smelly spick."

"I used to be beautiful. I could have had my pick of the guys up in Silicon Valley. All of the Internet startup millionaires, any one of them. There were ten guys to each girl there, and I was the best looking and I could have married any of them. Now I don't think anyone would want me."

"Plenty of guys would want you."

Those tears welled right back up to the point that both of her eyes were shiny with the water in them, but the tears never dropped out of her eyes.

"I don't think so. None worth having, anyhow. And I love him, too. I always thought that we'd settle down together and have kids someday."

"You might try to stick it out with him, you know."

"Oh, I know. He's got a good family, and his parents are rich, and he's got a good company. And he's got good friends like you, Jack. And he's got money. I don't have any money at all. I could have sued the bastard before him that made me have an abortion – sued him for mental abuse and gotten damages, but I just wanted to forget about that damned abortion. And I wanted to move in with David."

Again with the fake tears.

"Life is terrible. I bring these things on myself and I should know better. I'm a big girl. When I tell him how lousy he is he just screams profanities back at me and tells me what I should do to myself and where to stick it and where to go. Why can't he just give me a ring? I'd cook for him, I'd clean, and I'd do anything he wanted. I'd let him do whatever he wanted to do."

"I'm really sorry."
"Yes, I'm sorry too. Well there's nothing that we can do about it, is there? Let's get back to the bar."
"Becky, honestly, there's nothing I can do about it."
"Just don't let him know that we've talked all about this. I know he just wants to start and argument with me to give him an excuse. He just wants to make more money so that he can go and screw more sluts down in Newport. Don't think I don't know about those sluts Jack. All they care about is money."
"I don't think they're into him. He's not that kind of guy. He really isn't."
"Yes he is, that bastard. He's a sneaky guy, Jack. You can't trust him. And that's all he cares about is screwing those sluts and that's why he won't marry me. He wants to go on and screw all those girls."
"Want to get back to the bar?"
"Yes. Let's go."
We came back to the bar from a table around the way. The tears had dried up instantly. Grey sat with a smug smile as we joined him at the bar.
"What are you smiling at?" She glared at him.
"I'm smiling at you and all of your lies and rumors and bull…"
"I haven't told Jack any of your secrets. All of your friends will know soon enough. I just wanted to make sure that Jack heard my side of the story."
"What story? About you moving back north, back home?"
"Yes, about me going back to Cupertino. Oh Jack! I forgot to tell you. I'm going back home to Cupertino."
"That's nice."
"Yes, it will all be so nice and proper. With us living together, and all of this talk about getting married, and now

he's leaving me and I'm just moving back home. Just like it always happens. I'm going back to live with my parents. My parents don't know about it yet, either. And he's going to give me ten thousand dollars and pay off my credit card bills."

She stared at Grey's downcast eyes. He didn't look back at her. He wasn't smiling anymore.

"Ah, you weren't going to pay off the credit card? Thought I would just go away quietly without a fight? You have to settle all of your debts David. I want ten thousand dollars. You're such a nice guy. So giving."

How could people be so outright mean to each other? How could she say this to his face, and in front of me? And how could she say this to David Grey? He was such a nice guy, and his ego was so fragile and you could tell that the slightest thing would offend him. You would think that he would just run away and pull the trigger if you said certain things to him. And there she was spitting it at him.

"Can't we do this in private, Becky?"

"Can you believe this guy? I'm moving home. I'm going to live with my parents. Did you live with your parents after college? Well, they'll welcome me home all right, but it's not the same. You're not really wanted. And the rules. 'Can I go out mom?' 'What time will you be home?' 'Bye mom!' 'How's that David doing?' 'Oh he left her, better try and not mention it.' 'Poor poor Becky, she's the victim in all of this.' Sounds like fun to me. What do you think David? Sound like fun?

She was loving every moment of this speech. Now she had an audience.

"And David just goes on making money. Yes, it's all my fault; I know that I'm an insane bitch and that I'm too emotional. I know he thinks I'm crazy. Well at least I made you stop seeing all of your ex girlfriends. Yes, I knew about all of the sluts he was screwing behind my back. Well he has a small dick, and I'm sure none of them liked it and they were only doing it for his money."

"Why don't you shut up Becky?"

"Why? Don't you want your friend to know about all of the girls that you were screwing while we were together? And you guys go to the gym together; I'll bet he knows that you have a small dick. Well you loved your girlfriends, but when you met me I was the only thing in your little inexperienced world. Well I made him get rid of his ex wife, too. She was out from Boston and he was up in a hotel and I know he was with her. So after he screwed her I told him to come home on his cell phone. I made him tell her that he was going to run out and get something to eat. And he came straight home and never went back to her."

"You need to understand Jack, that he really is a terrible lover. And he hasn't got any balls when it comes to relationships. If you're going to break up with a girl you should just break up with her and not lead her on like you do David. Well, how can I expect anything less? He left his ex-wife for me, and he's going to leave me for all of those little sluts. And for his work. All about the mighty dollar, isn't it David? Well if it's so that your business can be a success, why not. It's all about your business. Well I hope you make yourself damn wealthy, and won't it all be worth it?"

"Are you listening to me David? Do you hear me? I know you can hear me but are you listening? I know you won't mind Jack hearing this. Do yourself a favor and don't get into fights with all of these sluts that you're planning on screwing. Because do you want to know something?

You're not very attractive when you fight. You're just a regular wife-beating stereotypical low class loser, fucking piece of shit blue-collar cop. Just break up with them and give it to them straight, but please, for your own good try not to get angry and explode with them because nobody likes a wife-beater. Just get a hold of yourself. Look at me David. Well I suppose we should all honor your career and get out of the way of a great young entrepreneur. Look, I'm even moving home to live with my parents with out a fuss. I'm going back to Cupertino. I'm doing it all for the young entrepreneur who will soon be captain of industry. Except that you're not exactly young, are you David? You're 36 – well, I guess that's young for a CEO. Look at Michael Dell, look at Steve Jobs. Look at Bill Gates. David doesn't think Bill Gates is very smart and that his products suck, but he never was very good with technology, good like you are, right David? If you're so smart, then why don't you have the money Bill Gates has? Do you think he has to dump his wife every time he needs a new business idea? What do you think he said to his girlfriends when he decided not to marry them? Do you think he tied them up with zip ties and told them so many low class things about themselves? I wonder if he has trouble getting hard like you do. Or maybe he doesn't even remember. Well David was so busy working on his business that he barely remembers living with me. I can tell you that much. Jack, where are you going?"

"I've got to go meet up with my friend Dwight."

Grey looked at me as I got up and said these things to Becky. I wondered why he let her make a scene. Why did he just keep his mouth shut like that? Why did he just sit there taking it?

THE 909

As I left the bar I glanced over my shoulder to see what was going on and she was just ranting and raving at him still. And even more animated about things. It looked like she was asking questions and punctuating them herself with "huh? .... huh? ..." I threw the bartender a twenty and told him thank you and sorry for my friends. When I pushed my way through the swinging door she was still bitching at him. I got in my car and turned the radio all the way up.

PART TWO

CHAPTER SEVEN

I parked my car in the garage and as I was walking up to my door Vanessa stopped me.

"Hey you. A couple of your friends were by here."

"Anyone you know? Did they leave a message for me?"

"It was the one who came in drunker than you know what last night, and what looks like her boyfriend. Are they rich or something?"

"Was she with one of my friends?"

"I didn't recognize him. But he looked like one of your friends. Very good looking, very well dressed, very stuck up. That girl, too. Were you ever with her? I think I've seen her over here. She's cute. Maybe you could introduce us? Just kiddin' Jack. I've never seen him around here before though."

Vanessa, like many other strippers I know is a lesbian, and open about it, and we joke about it. We both like girls. We have more in common than meets the eye.

"They didn't leave a message with you?"
"Oh, they told me that they would be back in an hour."
"If you see them, tell them I'll be up in my room and to just come in."

My stripper friend Vanessa had the unique opportunity as a person to be in very close contact with people, especially males, from all walks of life. She was fond of pointing out each of my friends that she would like to be better acquainted with. Male and female, of course – her tastes varied. She would also give me detailed commentary of their lives based on the shoes, watches, and clothes they were wearing, their hands, and other less couth aspects of their appearance. If she asked for an introduction, it was one in every hundred people that she met. She was impressed by me recent company. I know this because I got any message at all. Many of my less presentable looking friends have been given a hard time at my door – you had to pass Vanessa's door to get to mine and Vanessa's was always open, and she was always home except for times when she worked, and this was generally during times that nobody would stop by. So she regularly screened all of my guests and friends. One of my friends commented that if you wanted to get a hold of me you had better be nice to Vanessa.

I wondered what Kelley had done to Vanessa to make such an impression on her. But then I reminded myself how beautiful Kelley was. She didn't have to do anything. I checked my email and there was a message from Jason Steele that he would be coming in on a United Flight. I closed my email, threw my clothes in my closet and took a shower. I heard the doorbell ring, and so I quickly put on a robe I had stolen from the Ritz in Paris and went downstairs drying my hair with a towel. It was Kelley with Kevin at the door. Kevin had several bottles of liquor with him.

"Hello there sweetheart," Kelley said, "Are you going to invite us in?"

"Come in, come in. Please. I was just in the shower."

"Oh that sounds wonderful. We've been up all night."

"Kevin, come have a seat. What can I get you to drink? Beer? Water? Coke?"

"I don't know if you like this sort of thing, Jack, but I brought you some of my favorite from France. It's called Chartreuse."

"Let me get some of these fixed up," and Kelley took the bottle.

"Get me some ice and some glasses, Jack." I brought in three small tumblers with ice in from the kitchen. Kelley set out uncorking the Chartreuse and poring the drinks.

"What a day. What a night."

"You don't remember Duane's, our lunch today?"

"No, were we supposed to meet up today? I'll feel terrible. I must have been totally obliterated when you asked me."

"You were pretty drunk," Kevin said.

"Oh, you're right. Kevin's been such a peach."

"You made quite an impression on Vanessa out there."

"I should have, I gave her a hundred bucks."

"You've got to be kidding me."

"I thought we should do something nice for waking her up last night."

"He's so thoughtful that way," Kelley said, "And he always remembers everything when we drink."

"So do you, Kelley."

"Yeah right," Kelley said. "I don't remember anything. Hey, what about those drinks?"

"Hey, fix the rest of this up while I go put some clothes on. The ice is in the freezer."
"Okay."

I went upstairs and put on some jeans, a black t shirt and some black leather wingtips. As I was combing my hair I could hear Kelley and Kevin downstairs laughing and clinking glasses and shaking drinks with ice. I could hear her bumping up the stairs and she came into my bathroom while I was combing my hair, taking my time.
"How are you doing baby? Little hung over?" And she kissed me perfunctorily on the cheek.
"I'm in love with you Kelley."
"Baby," she said. "Do you want me to get rid of him?"
"Kevin? No. I really like him."
"I'll tell him to take off."
"Don't do that."
"Yeah, I'll tell him to go back to the hotel."
"You can't do that Kelley."
"Just watch me. He'll do anything I tell him to do. He's got it bad for me, I'm telling you."

She walked back downstairs and I quit looking at myself in the mirror in the bathroom and flopped face down onto my bed. The white down comforter felt cool and made a nice sound as I fell face first down onto the bed. I felt terrible. I could hear them talking downstairs but I had no idea what they were saying.
"Poor baby," she was running her fingers through my hair.
"What did you say?" I looked away from her, and I couldn't stand to look at her.
"He's on his way to the grocery store to pick up some booze. He loves good booze."
"Do you feel any better? Do you have a headache?"
"I'm alright."

"Shhhhh. It'll be alright. He's going downtown."
"Can't we just be together, Kelley?"
"You know how I am, Jack. I would just ruin you with all of the men. I love you too much to do that do you."
"You do it to me now."
"It would be different if we were together. I'm sorry, it's just the way I am."
"We could run away to Europe or some tropical island somewhere."
"Don't even go there. You know I would go in a second. But I couldn't just fade away into obscurity. I've got family here. A good job."
"Yeah."
"You've always been my white knight. You know that you're the yardstick by which I measure all of the men I meet. You're my true love. Anyhow, enough of that bullshit. I'm going to get out of town for a while, Jack, and then Jon B's coming back."
"Why are you taking off?"
"It'll be good for both of us. Out of sight, out of mind."
"When?"
"As soon as possible. Today."
"Where?"
"La Quinta."
"We should go together."
"I thought we already went over this Jack."
"I never agreed with you."
"That's crap Jack. Don't be a moron, baby."
"Easy for you to say. Anyhow, you're right. It's just when I'm depressed that I talk this way. When I'm depressed, I'm a complete moron."

    I got up off my bed and straightened my shirt out. I was still depressed.

"Don't look at me like that Jack."
"How do you want me to look at you?"
"Don't make me sick. I'm leaving tonight anyhow."
"Tonight?"
"Isn't that what I just said? Yes, I am leaving tonight."
"Well let's have that drink."
"Yes, let's. And Kevin will be back any minute now. He's good about finding good things to drink."

We went back downstairs and into the living room where I had some old single malted whiskey. I poured each of us a small shot and we drank them slowly. The doorbell rang and it was Kevin with ice, some strange looking bottles, lemons, and assorted groceries.
"Where should I put this stuff?"
"Over there in the kitchen by the sink," I said.
"Kelley, please get me a blender. I hope you don't mind, Jack. I have a secret recipe that I picked up in Peru for this chilled drink that you'll never forget."
"You're always bringing back recipes from other countries," Kelley said, "Where do you get these recipes? What is her name this time?"
"A rather pretty Japanese tourist this time."
"Wow, another date. We all have our friends, don't we Kevin? Our dates? Why don't you have many dates these days, Jack?"
"I promise you, Jack," Kevin reassured me with a pat on the back, "The grass is always greener. There's always something else in the world. Good to find a good woman and stick with her."
"I don't know, I've gotten all sorts of things from my different friends."
"Let's get that blender, Kevin."

THE 909

Kevin was looking at Kelley sitting on the couch and her cigarette ash was about an inch long.

"Let me get that cigarette Kelley." She saw me notice the ashes that we're falling on my furniture.

I brought in some ashtrays from the kitchen and put one on the coffee table in front of the couch that Kelley was sitting at. Kevin brought out an orange cigar box with two cigars in it and offered me one.

"Let me finish my cigarette."

"Some Cubans I brought home with me from Honk Kong. You should try one."

He brought out a gold cutter from his pocket and quickly snapped to slice off a very thin bit that he puffed lightly while roasting and lighting the other end of the cigar to produce and even burn.

"I love a really fresh cigar. Most of the cigars you get aren't fresh, and they're not stored properly. You need to keep these in a humidor."

"When you get married Kelley -- won't you still have your boyfriends?"

"I know. I'm terrible."

"No, you won't need all of them anymore. You'll find one good man. A rich one."

"Thanks, Kevin."

"I'm not kidding. You're the most beautiful girl I've ever known. Your body. You've got the look. Incredible, really. You make men insane with desire. I'm not kidding, either Kelley, you are stunning. And this is one thing I never joke about. Jack knows me. I never kid about women. If you start kidding around about women, people think you don't have any class."

"I know," said Kelley, "I kid around about men all of the time and most people think I'm trash. Everyone except Jack here. He knows I'm a good girl."
"You don't talk to Jack about other men?"
"No," said Kelley, "I wouldn't talk with him about that."
"Ah," said Kevin, "You don't talk to him at all then?"
"I hate this conversation. Let's drink. How about a martini?"
"You're always loaded." Kevin said, "How about we just relax for a while? Besides when you're drunk we can never talk seriously. Jack and I need to talk about women for a while."

I went back over to the kitchen and poured three of the drinks that Kevin had concocted in the kitchen. I added a bit more ice to the blender, jabbed at the blend button a bit, and then brought the blender pitcher and three glasses back into the living room.
"I would really like to hear you talk about men sometime Kelley."
"That's an interesting idea," Kelley said. She sipped at her drink and twirled the glass around to make the ice clink against each other and the glass.
"Isn't he insane?" Kelley asked.
"Now let's drink," Kevin said.

I held my glass up in a mock salute and we all sipped at our drinks.
"I only truly love Asian women. Their bodies represent the ideal body type, even into their forties and fifties. They have truly wonderful bodies."
"Go ahead and get yourself an Asian woman then," Kelley said.
"I just might."

Kevin had a point about Asian women.

"You ought to write a book about women some time, Kevin."

"All I want out of women is to enjoy them, Mr. Baker."

"Let's enjoy a little more of that drink you made up Kevin," Kelley said. She pushed her glass towards Kevin and he poured more of the contents of the blender into her glass. He moved with such elegance, and he poured very carefully.

"So Jack," he filled my glass.

"Kelley tells me you know your way around the world. I hear you have been all over. Ever been to Italy?"

"I was there last year."

"Do you know where Kevin was last year?" Kelley asked.

"In prison. And I've got the scars to prove it. Have you ever seen a shank wound before?"

Kevin stood up, unbuttoned his jeans, and pulled up his shirt. He pulled his undershirt out of his pants and stood there, with impressive and obviously strong tanned abdominal muscles. He had a good body and little body hair.

"See those scars there?"

"Nice."

"It didn't hurt very much, either. I ended up making this guy my bitch."

"How did you get stabbed?"

"In a holding cell, being moved out to the country club. That was when I was mixed in with the riff-raff."

"What did you do again, Kevin? Hacking? Computer Stuff?" Kelley asked. "Were you really working with the Mafia?"

"It never did anything for money. Just personal interest."

"I told you he was one of us, Jack." Kelley said. "You're so awesome Kevin. I love you so much."

"You're sweet Kelley. But don't lie to me."
"Don't be a jackass."
"See, Jack. The only way I can appreciate the finer things in life is because I've been so low. You have to hit bottom. Once you've really lived and experienced the bad, only then can you truly appreciate how good things can get. Don't you think so?"
"Absolutely."
"I agree. And the most important thing to appreciate in life is a woman. I love women."
"Don't you ever fall in love with just one woman?"
"Every time, Kelley. I am always in love with exactly one woman."
"So how does that affect your appreciation for women?"
"It does a great deal for my appreciation for women."
"You're a player. You haven't got any morals."
"Actually you're wrong. I've got plenty of morals."

We drank the rest of Kevin's magic concoction and he left the bottles and fixings in my kitchen. We ate at Gerard's, the nicest and only French restaurant in Riverside. It was an excellent dinner. Kevin also had an excellent appreciation for food. And also for alcohol. You could be sure that they were a strong part of his morals. Kevin was animated and laughed during our meal. We had a great time.
"Where to now?" Kevin asked after we were finished.
"Let's go back downtown. We've had such a good time here." We had closed Gerard's and the staff was milling around waiting for us to finish up. You could tell they wanted to leave. We were the last people there.
Kevin was laughing. He was having a good time.

"I think we're all socially compatible," he said. He was smoking the second Cuban. "Why aren't you two together or married or something?"
"I'm not a one woman man," I said.
"He's always working," she said, "let's get out of here."
"Let's have a Port," Kevin said.
"Let's have it downtown."
"No, let's have it here where we can talk."
"You and your talking," said Kelley. "Why do men always want to talk?"
"Isn't it women who always want to talk?" said Kevin.
"Waiter!" Kevin said.
"Sir."
"What is the finest Port wine you have?"
"I think we have the '94 Fonseca."
"Bring us that bottle, please."
"Kevin, you don't have to do that."
"Believe me Kelley. I appreciate wine more than many of the other things I appreciate."
"I wonder: How often do you appreciate these things?"
"Great ones all the time."

We finally made it to downtown Riverside. Mario's was packed with people. Their conversations all hit you in pieces as you walked in. There was a jazz quartet and they were swinging. I swung Kelley around the bar for a while. There was some guy that recognized Kelley and waved at her.
"You never called me."
"I'm not interested."
"Bitch."

The guy couldn't take a hint.
"Friend of mine," Kelley said. "Guy can't take a hint."

The jazz stopped for a second and we saw Kevin over at a table with three Asian girls. We headed over to his table when the band started back up and we were swept up in the music again. I spun her around a few times.
"You can't dance Jack. Jon's the best dancer in the world."
"He's a good guy."
"He's wonderful"
"I like Jon," I said. "I like that guy."
"I'm going to marry him someday," Kelley said. "I haven't thought of him since he left."
"Don't you call him or send him at least one email a day?"
"No."
"He calls you all the time."
"I never pick up. Caller ID. I never check my voice mail. It's full."
"When are you guys going to get married?"
"Who knows? As soon as he dumps all of his girlfriends and I get my divorce paid for."
"Any way I can help?"
"No. Jon's rich. His people are rich."

The band was taking a break between sets now so we walk back over to Kevin's table and join him with his Asian women.
"You look brilliant, Kelley," he said.
"Why didn't you come out there?" I asked.
"How can I dance with three girls at once?"
"We'll show you next time baby," Kelley said.
"Don't tempt me Kelley. I would destroy your innocence."
"Sounds good to me. Any time. What about your friends? Are they in on this game?"
"I'll tell you this – they're my women, but I wouldn't want them around together when we're together."
"This guy isn't messing around, is he?"

"Not at all, no. He's not. I'm not sure I agree with him though."

"Jack is a pervert that way. He likes to watch."

"He does, does he?"

"Let's go cut a rug," Kelley said.

We went back to the dance floor and held each other. Her skin was smooth beneath her dress and it felt good to dance with her so close.

"Baby," Kelley said, " I'm so depressed."

This was starting to sound familiar. "You seemed OK back at the table. Do you want another drink?"

The band struck up a tune that everyone in the bar had heard before and so everyone was clapping and hollering and cheering.

"Life is so empty."

"What are you talking about?"

"It just sucks."

The chorus of the song broke over us and everyone in the crowd was going wild.

"Let's get out of here."

I knew this was leading me back to a place that I had been before, a bad place. But I wanted desperately to get back there again.

"… and forevermore …," the band sang.

"Let's get out of here." Kelley said, "Is that OK with you?"

"Kelley isn't feeling so well, " I said to Kevin. He grinned and said, "I'm sorry to hear that. You take care of her now."

"We had a great time. I don't suppose you're going to let me pick up this tab."

And Kevin just waved his hand over the check in a horizontal karate chop and said don't worry about it.

We left the bar and Kelley went to the bathroom before we left Mario's and headed toward the car.

Kelley came back from the bathroom and gave Kevin a kiss on the check and a hug – her standing up and him sitting down. When we walked out of the door there were still several girls at his table.

I drove her around the way to her hotel and we held hands in the car during the ride. And the time I wasn't shifting her legs felt wonderful over her black nylon stockings.

"Stay," she said when we arrived and didn't want me to come up to her room.

I got out of the car to walk her to her door.

"Are you serious?"

"Yes, please don't. I mean no, don't come."

"Good night. Sorry you're feeling so bad. Talk to you later."

"Good night Jack – we can't do this ever again." We started kissing and she felt good and I backed her up against the wall. We were tearing each other apart. We kissed some more in her room and she suddenly stopped. Her hair was a mess and her clothes were messed up and she told me to leave.

She stood up and locked herself in the bathroom and I could hear her crying. I left the room so she couldn't hear the door shut when I closed it. I drove home and went to sleep.

CHAPTER EIGHT

I didn't see Kelley again until she came back from the desert. She did send me a postcard with a picture of a golf course on the back. It said, "Very dry, very hot, very nice. Say hello to the guys for me. Love KH."
I didn't see David Grey either. I heard that Becky had moved home and I got an email from Grey saying that he was going to visit his family in Orange County, didn't know where he was going to stay, but he wanted to make sure we were still on for the trip to the desert we had talked about in the winter. The best way to get a hold of him was though his mom.
Kelley was nowhere to be seen, I had Grey out of my hair, and it was nice to get them all out of my system. It was nice not having to go to the gym. Business was good and I had plenty of clients to deal with. I was working to get ahead for my trip with Jason to go rock climbing. Jason was in town for two days before leaving for Santa Cruz where he would stay with his uncle for three weeks. He left to go see his uncle who is a famous herbalist and writer up

in Santa Cruz. He and his uncle and found some verbena and also ate some great mushrooms that tasted like steak with A1 sauce on them. Jason had made some serious money as a contractor living and working in Las Vegas and it was good to have him home. He was just back from Santa Cruz now for our trip to Palm Desert. And then he sent me an email that said, "See you Monday."

Monday night he showed up. I heard his truck pull in the driveway and I went outside to say hello. I grabbed one of his bags from the back and we walked inside.

"It sounds like you had a great trip."

"The best," he said. "Santa Cruz was awesome."

"How was Chris?"

"He's great. He has a new baby boy. Named him after grandpa."

"And how was the city?"

"Good and bad. Well pretty bad actually. I'm not sure I remember too much of it. And I slept too much."

"You probably needed the rest. How was the nightlife?"

"Nightlife bad. Really bad. And I was really, really high."

He was talking about smoking.

"How did that happen? Let's have a martini. You have a head start on me."

Jason blinked his eyes hard and shook his head. "It's insane," he said. "Chris had some mushrooms that he picked up in Oregon. Suddenly we were really very high."

"How long?"

"The whole week. We were high for a week."

"What did you do?"

"I really don't remember. Didn't eat any meat. I think I sent you an email. I remember that."

"Did you do anything else?"

"I don't know! Seriously."

THE 909

"Just start from the beginning."
"It's all a blur. It's a series of visions and scenes that run all together. I can't remember."
"Drink that beer and remember. Let's go."
"O.K. it's coming back to me," Jason said. I remember something about a dark bar in Santa Cruz and a nice lesbian. Could have been bisexual. That I can remember."
"O.K."
"Beautiful. She was very beautiful. Blonde. She looked like Charlise Theron and was telling me how she likes things nasty. All of a sudden people where throwing punches. I wasn't involved. This girl had just dumped her girlfriend. Out looking for trouble. Everyone in the bar knows her and talking to me in a big scandal. Then butch ex-girlfriend comes around the bar and starts fight with the first person stupid enough to talk back to her. Then everyone was involved. Lesbians were running around everywhere, yelling and shoving one another, being loud and violent. I can remember that. The pretty lesbian came home with me in my car. Her ride was gone. Couldn't get her things from her friend's car. They threw everyone out of the bar. O.K. it's all coming back to me now."
"Did you hang out with her?"
"Went to my place. Loaned the lesbian a couple of bucks for a cab and went back to the bar with her to try to find her ride. She thought that maybe they had gone back home without her. More drinks. Can't remember if I paid for them or if she did."
"I'm sure it was you."
"Yeah, logic would prove you right. Yes, I paid. That's right."
"So how did things end up?"

"Nothing. No hook up. We spent all night looking for her ride and finally they drive by and tell her we're going home. She goes. She thanks me."

"What ever happened to her? Did you get her number or email?"

"She's a programmer. Nice big home up in the hills. She's going to send me an email and I'll stay at her place the next time I'm in Santa Cruz."

"You'll have better luck next time."

"We'll see. Anyhow, let's eat," Jason said, "unless you want me to keep it up with the stories."

"Tell me more."

"Let's eat. I'm hungry."

We walked down to the driveway and into my car. It was finally cooling down to 90 – a typical June in Riverside.

"Where we going?"

"Let's eat at the Bluffs."

"Cool."

We shot up Cooley and right on Washington down past the concrete ice skating rink.

"An ice skating rink," Jason said. "Want to check it out? Do some ice-skating?"

"Man, you're messed up." He had been drinking vodka martinis.

"Pretty good ice skating they have there on the cement."

"Uh huh."

"You could glide free as a bird over there on your roller, I mean your ice skates. Be a blast. And cheap, too. Five bucks a throw for an experience you'll never forget. You wont forget, will you?"

"We'll do it after dinner."

"OK, OK. That's cool. Road to Riverside paved with un-ice-skated-on-concrete."

THE 909

    We pulled into The Bluffs on Washington.
"I didn't know you were a big ice-skater."
"I always loved figure skating. Could have gone pro. A regular Jason Harding. Watch your knees sucker."
    We went into the bar first and had another round of martinis. We both had a good start.
"I love being messed up at night," Jason said. "You should give it a try."
"You're about four hundred and twenty ahead of me."
"Don't let that get you down. Turn that frown upside down. Just don't lose it. Never lose it in public. I never did lose it in public."
"Where were you drinking before you got in?"
"Stopped in over at Lake Alice. Dwight was just about to lose it. He hasn't scored for about a week."
"He'll be back in business soon."
"Yeah he'll be cool. I just wish he would get back to work."
"What do you want to do tonight?"
"Let's take it easy. Do they have any scrambled egg whites here?" If they had any decent food around here we wouldn't have to drive all the way to Irvine to get something to eat.
"Negative," I said. "Let's eat a real dinner."
"Just an idea," Jason said. "Let's do this."
"Let's go."
    We went outside to smoke a cigarette. Most of the newspaper machines were empty. I ate here for breakfast regularly and I knew that they were empty because they never filled them in the first place.
"Shit! Did you see that girl? She just got out of the concrete ice-skating rink. I'm going to send all of my friends gift

certificates to go ice skating on concrete for Christmas this year."

    A cab pulled into the driveway as we were smoking our cigarettes. Someone inside waved at us and you could see her lean forward to tap on the driver's shoulder. The cab pulled over to the curb and the door slammed shut. It was Kelley.

"Oh my god is she the bomb."
"Hey" Kelley said. "How are you doing?"
"This is Jason. Kelley Taylor."

    Jason smiled at Kelley.

"Wow, I just flew back. Haven't even been home yet."
"Come have a drink with us before you go home."
"We're going to the Red Fox, then" Kelley said, "I love their martinis."

    Kelley looked at Jason.

"Have you been in Riverside long?"
"I just got back from Santa Cruz today."
"How was Santa Cruz?"
"Excellent Santa Cruz was excellent."
"Ask him about the lesbians."
"Lesbians," said Jason, "don't understand lesbians. Actually, yes I do understand lesbians. I'm a riot girl. I'm very punk."
"Very much like straight people. Very much like people here. You're about as punk as people here are cool."
"Exactly. Just like us here."
"You guys have quite a head start on me."

    Sitting at the bar of the Red Fox we all had another martini.

"How are you Jack?"
"Great. Everything's going well."

THE 909

Kelley looked directly at me. "I was stupid to leave," she said. "Everyone comes back home to the 909, don't they?"
"Did you have an OK time?"
"You can say that. OK. Nothing too interesting."
"Did you see anyone from back home?"
"No, I barely ever left my hotel room."
"You didn't even go down to the pool?"
"Nope. Didn't do hardly anything."
"Sounds like the 909."
Kelley's eyes smiled at Jason.
"So that's what happened in Santa Cruz."
"It was all about Santa Cruz."
Kelley smiled at Jason again.
"I like your friends, Jack. You always have the best friends."
"He's a good guy. A professional ice skater. And stay away from him."
"Only when I'm up the street. And I'm actually a professional concrete ice skater." Jason said.
"I'll have one more martini," Kelley said, "and then I have to go home and take a bath. Have the waitress call a cab for me."
"There's yours from earlier. He's waiting for you."
"Obviously." Kelley said.
We finished our round and walked Kelley out to the cab.
Make sure to be at Mario's at eleven. Jon's going to be there so make sure Jason comes.
"We'll be there, Jason said. "She's a good one. Who's Jon?"
"The guy she's going to marry."

"Shit. Lucky bastard. All of the good ones are married or taken. What should I give them for their wedding? Maybe a couple of gift certificates to go ice-skating on the concrete?"

"We need to eat dinner."

"Is that girl Kelley, *the* Kelley Taylor?"

"Oh yes. That Kelley Taylor. Country clubs, Mercedes, the whole nine."

"Lucky bastard."

We finally ended up at Akina sushi over in Riverside for something to eat. It was packed with locals who craved real ethnic experiences outside of the breakfast at the International House of Pancakes. Some soul had taken the great risk of putting a Japanese food restaurant in the middle of Moreno Valley and the place had been doing well ever since. It was a big deal to drink booze with the sushi chefs, like they do in Los Angeles. And to have your own bottle of sake waiting for you. We had some good tuna, yellow tail, and went to the Teppan grill after that for teriyaki chicken and steak. And the shrimps that he threw into our mouths. We both caught the shrimps he threw at us.

After the sushi, teriyaki, Asahi's and several large sakes later we got the bill and left the place. We had parked the car back by the movie theatre and on our walk back to the car we noticed how dry and hot the wind was. There was dust blowing from new housing developments in the area.

"Those houses up on those hills there. 10,000 square feet for three hundred grand."

"That's it? That wouldn't buy you a shack in Orange County."

"That's what I'm talking about. Live the good life here or live like a beggar in Irvine."
We walked for about five minutes admiring the view of the city lights and of Box Springs Canyon Mountain off in the distance. The radio towers and aviation beacons blinked brightly in the crisp clean, hot air of the desert.
"I love the desert. Nice to be back home," Jason said.
We smoked a couple of cigarettes out by my car, leaning up against it for support and to get in out of the wind a bit.
"Should we have another round?"
"I'm fine."
We got in the car and made a left onto Allesandro. Then right down Canyon Crest, even though there were likely several speed traps and a huge hill that you couldn't avoid going 100 miles an hour down. And at eleven or twelve in the evening there was always the danger of getting stopped at sobriety checkpoints. We drove by a fraternity house that was obviously winding up for the night. The sorority license plate framed cars were slowly arriving.
"What do you want to do? Do you want to stop in and see Kelley and Jon?"
"Sure."
We drove over to Chicago and then up University. Passing the vacant properties and old brick buildings we made a right onto Lime and parked. We walked up toward the Mission Inn, which is right across the street from Mario's and we saw Kelley and Jon sitting at a table by the bar. Jon got up to meet us at the door and Kelley stayed behind.
"Hey Jack! How are you?"
"Very well, and yourself?"
"Oh, I'm doing alright. Just got back from Peru and Costa Rica."

Jason had gone into the bar and was sitting at the table with Kelley.

"It's good to see you, Jack," Jon said. "I've had a few beers. Insane. Do you see my face getting all red?"

"Let's go see Kelley. You have an amazing body. Where did you get that?"

"A guy sent it from the bar."

"That's a god awful drink. Get yourself a good drink."

"Oh we drink so many martinis these days."

"I haven't met Jason yet. You're such a thoughtful host Jack."

Kelley turned to Jason. "This is Jason. This drunk bastard over here is Jon Boswell. Jonathan Boswell is a convicted felon."

"Aren't I? The damn FBI and their ego."

"What did you just say?"

"Ran into them at a bar in San Francisco the other night. They wanted to gloat over me for putting me away. They came over and said hello. Kelley, you do have the most beautiful body I have ever seen on a woman. Don't you guys think she's hot?"

"Beautiful? These little things?"

"They're fun bags. Go ahead and show us. Aren't they wonderful, gentlemen?"

"You should have stayed in San Francisco, Jon."

"OK, OK, let's go to bed early tonight."

"Oh my god I can't wait." Kelley said.

"You need to learn to treat women with respect – we're in mixed company here dear."

"Seriously, doesn't she have the most beautiful body you've ever seen?" Jon said.

"Let's go to our place and watch the Sopranos," Jason said. They're bringing back Tony's mother.

"Yes, that's a great idea" – Jon was ahead of us on the drinking and he was trying to get his act together "but Kelley and I have a date to finish up here. Kelley, take your top off."

Kelley slapped him playfully on the face pretending to be serious but then she held Jon around the shoulders and gave everyone a sheepish smile, but one that let us all know that it was OK if we broke the party up and went home.

"You are so beautiful. I can't believe it, oh my god you're beautiful."

We waved goodbye and we all shook hands and gave each other hugs.

"I'm really sorry I can't make it with you guys, but you know, previous engagements," Jon said. Kelley and everyone else were laughing uncontrollably. When we were all but out the door of the bar I looked back in to see Jon and Kelley at the bar laughing and having fun. Kelley looked slightly aloof, but Jon's hands were all over her and you could tell she didn't hate it.

Walking to our car I asked Jason: "You really want to go back home and watch some tube?"

"Yes," said Jason. "So long as we have something to eat back there other than Del Taco."

"Jon was pretty happy with his woman there," I said when we were both in the car and after I had gotten it started."

"Well you know buddy she is god damn gorgeous."

CHAPTER NINE

The Sopranos episodes we watched back at home were good and entertaining. We stayed up too late – until about three or four in the morning. When I woke up I checked my email and found a note sent from David Grey, which was sent from an Internet service provider in Palm Desert. I checked the headers. You can usually tell exactly where someone sends a email from if you know where to look. He was enjoying the finest things that life had to offer, he said, golfing, swimming and getting a good tan, and going out on the town. When were we coming out there? Can I pick him up some earplugs for the concert? He would reimburse me the expense when I arrived in Palm Desert.

I wrote him back after checking the rest of my email and having breakfast that Jason and I would leave Riverside at the end of the week. And he said that unless I sent him further email to the contrary, we would meet in Palm Desert on the 6th and then drive on together to Joshua Tree for some rock climbing. That evening I went over to

THE 909

Mario's to see Jon and Kelley, but they weren't there so I went over to Lake Alice where they were drinking beer.
"Hi baby doll," Kelley came over and hugged me.
"Hi Jack," Jon said. "Was I hammered last night or what?"
"Oh yes," Kelley said. "Absolutely messed up."
"Hey," Jon said. "Where are you guys leaving for the desert? You wouldn't mind if we tagged along, would you?"
"That would be awesome."
"Seriously, you're alright with us hanging around? I've been once, but Kelley's never been and are you sure we won't put a cramp in your style?"
"Don't even start. It's fine."
"I'm pretty buzzed, so I wouldn't even bring it up if I wasn't. You're sure it's alright?"
"Enough already," Kelley said. "He wouldn't tell you the truth anyway. I'll ask him about the details later."
"Seriously, it's all right, then?"
"Ask me again and I'll be pissed. Jason and I will be there on the morning of the 7th. We're going climbing for a couple of days before we settle in for the show."
"By the way, where is Jason at right now?" Kelley asked.
"He's drinking beer and smoking cigarettes with our neighbor Norm and his friend Jim."
"He's a good guy that Jason."
"Yes, I really like him. Funny, and smart – sometimes I don't catch the references he jokes about."
"You don't even remember him, Jon." Kelley said, "you're just repeating what I told you earlier."
"That's crap. I remember him perfectly. OK, Jack, we'll meet you down in Palm Desert the evening of the 7th. You know how Kelley is with getting an early start."
"I'm a vampire."

"That is, when my check comes and if you're sure we're still invited."
"We'll get the money, I'm sure of that. I'm not sure if we're welcome or not."
"Just be sure to bring gear for Joshua Tree – rugged shoes and et cetera."
"I won't do any climbing," Kelley said.
"Just bring yourselves, something to eat, and some warm clothes for the evening. Remember these desert nights get cold?"
"Isn't it going to be fun? Palm Desert and Joshua Tree? I can't wait!"
"The 7th, isn't that coming up?"
"It's next weekend."
"We'll have to get our act together."
"I'm going to the mall."
"I've got to take a shower," Kelley said. "Walk me to our hotel Jack, would ya?"
"Oh yeah, it's the nicest hotel I've ever stayed in. Much like the George V in Paris. They have hourly rates!"
"They were taken aback when we told them that we'd be staying the whole day, and night!"
"They cater to the local crowd. Specifically they cater to the crowd that hangs out by the Winchel's. I'm pretty familiar with that whole crowd, come to mention it."
"Get out of here and go to the mall, you ass."
Jon took off and left Kelley and I sitting at the bar.
"Another drink?"
"Maybe."
"Ah, I feel much better now."
We took a walk up University smoking cigarettes.
"It's been a while since we've seen each other," Kelley said.

"Yup."
"How are you doing Jack?"
"Alright."
  Kelley remembered something. "Hey Jack," she said, "is David Grey going with you on your trip?"
"Yeah. I think so."
"Do you think he's going to be cool about things?"
"What do you mean?"
"Who do you think I went out to La Quinta with, Jack?"
"Oh," I said. "Good for you."
I blew the smoke from my cigarette out sideways and quick.
"Why are you acting that way?"
"What is there to say? How should I act?"
  We hit the end of the good part of town and turned around.
"He was a good boy, but a bit boring."
"Was he, now?"
"Well I thought it was just what he needed."
"And you should know."
"Don't even go there."
"Alright, alright."
"You didn't know?"
"No. I didn't give it one thought."
"Do you think he'll be alright? Do you think he'll be cool with Jon around?"
"Not sure – that's all him. Just tell him you'll be there. He can always flake."
  I didn't hear from Kelley until the day before we were set to leave.
"So did you talk to Grey?"
"Yeah, he's still coming. Says he can't wait."
"Oh shit."

"I was pretty surprised to hear that myself."
"And he can't wait to see me."
"Did you tell him you'd be with Jon?"
"I told him that we're all coming down together – the whole group."
"What a guy."
"I know."

They were waiting for a check to come, and for their credit card balance to reflect recent payments. We would all meet in Palm Desert. They would drive directly from Riverside on the 10 freeway via the 60 through Moreno Valley and Beaumont to Palm Desert. We would all meet at the Mariott in Palm Desert. If they didn't turn up before Monday evening, we would head out to Joshua Tree for our climbing. We would rent motorcycles and ride these to Joshua Tree, and I left a rough itinerary for them so that they could follow us if they wanted to.

Jason and I woke up very early in the morning and set out down the 215 freeway. The morning was crisp and clean and you could tell that it would be a hot day in Colton. We stopped at the Bluffs for breakfast. I asked the waitress how long it would take us to get to Palm Springs, as if I wasn't from around here and we didn't know and she told me a couple of hours. We decided that we'd make a high speed run out to Cabazon and either eat at the outlet mall or at Hadley's Orchard's, which are next door to one another out in the middle of nowhere. We opted for the frozen Chinese-food-out-of-the-bag-and-into-the-fryer place at the outlet mall. Sitting all around us were some overweight people shoveling down fried foods and I'm sure several of these people took major advantage to the local all-you-cat-eat joints. I asked the guy behind the Chinese food counter if this was authentic Chinese food. He didn't understand my request and looked confused. I tried several times to ask him if this was the type of food that people ate in China.

I know what kind of food they eat in China, and it's nothing like what you get at the busy bee, whatever express. The Chinese wouldn't recognize the food as being theirs. I was in Hong King a couple of years ago and when I ordered Chicken soup I got a chop of a vivisection of a chicken in some broth. Feathers, lungs, guts, everything. I ended up eating rice and drinking beer across China.
"Where are you boys headed?" a big middle-aged lady asked us. "You don't look like you're from around here."
"The desert," I said.
"Ooooooo. That sounds wonderful. My cousin has a time share out in Palm Springs."
"Mmmmm. Palm Springs is NICE!" I said enthusiastically.
"That's just the thing you boys should be doing. Go out and have some fun."
"And what are you doing here?"
"Good God," Jason whispered to me.
"We're shopping at the outlets. There's a new Ralph Lauren store out here that sells seconds."
"That sounds great! Any good bargains?"
"Oh yes!"
"I love these consumers. Absolutely inspiring."
"Eat up all that good fried food. Mmm."
"What part are you boys from?"
"Riverside. He's from Rancho Cucamonga."
"And you're both headed out to Palm Springs?"
"We're going rock climbing in Joshua Tree first."
"Oh, I never did like it out there. It's so dry and hot. And with nothing to do out there. And rock climbing, how dangerous. I don't know anyone that's tried it. But don't

all those people go out there to Joshua tree and bang on drums and smoke dope?"

"I think that was back in the sixties ma'am."

We ate the broccoli beef and the orange chicken and the fried rice and noodles, and downed our large cokes. We felt the wind whip by and the sun beat down. At Hadley's we stopped in and bought a couple of bottles of water and I got a date shake. Back in the car we tuned into public radio and listened to some footage of the US senate talking about going to war with Iraq and president Bush. 89.3 KPCC came in out here and it was a miracle. All the best radio programming in Riverside – like DJ Tina Bold on the college radio station was out of range.

The drive to Palm desert was a fast, dry, high-speed run and we finally pulled off to the Marriott Desert Springs. As we pulled up the long line of palms and the oasis of greenery it felt good to see the luxury of the hotel. Waiting for us at the valet stand was David Grey. The valet opened our doors and started to unload the luggage from the trunk.

"Hello there Jack, how was your drive?"

"O.K.," I said. "This is Jason."

"Good to meet you."

"Let's go to my room, I've got some beer." Grey wasn't wearing his glasses and you could see him squint in the light. He was trying to get a good look at Jason. He was acting nervous, too. The kind of nervous that is contagious.

"Let's go to my room, it's really very nice."

We walked through the lobby, saying hello to the old parrots that they have had there for about thirty years. The valet told us he'd store our things before our suite was ready. He would call us in David's room when things were taken care of.

THE 909

"I'm really glad to finally meet you," David said to Jason. "I've heard all of the stories about you. Did you get my harness, Jack?"

We arrived at David's room and he opened the door and we went in for a couple of minutes. The concierge called about a minute later before we could get comfortable or have a beer so we left Grey in his room, and got a chance to unwind alone in our suite.

CHAPTER TEN

We woke up the next morning and the sun came in through the dark hotel curtains. We went downstairs to the café for breakfast. The air in the room was dry and it hurt your nose to breathe. The Marriott is a nice hotel. It's very clean and has a river running through it with boats that carry you to all of the different restaurants. Walking around outside the hotel early in the morning it was already hot. Too hot for golf or anything else that required activity. We walked around the grounds, past the pool, and then back up to our air-conditioned room.

I wasn't confident that we could find a sporting goods store that sold the equipment that we would need for our climbs in Joshua tree. I wanted to make sure we had a couple of new ropes, and also several other pieces of equipment to replace the items I have had for many years that should be replaced periodically. And Grey didn't have anything.

We went back downstairs to see what was going on at the pool. Grey started explaining to us where they got all of the reclaimed water for the golf courses, and I forget where he said it came from. The green grass and landscaping seemed nice to me. Then we went over to the bar to ask when the live bands would be here and they said that they usually started at about one o'clock or thereabouts. So we milled around a bit taking in the scenery and went over to the main bar to have a beer. We were going to pick up the gear later and we had eaten breakfast so we had time to stop in at the main bar to have a couple of beers. The sun was hot but the bar had water misters running and there was a dry but steady breeze blowing through the patio and was nice sitting and drinking our beer. There were some gulls around flying over the Spanish tiled estates surrounding the hotel and I didn't want to move from my seat at the bar. But we had to get going to pick up that gear before the shop closed. We paid for the beer. Jason and I split the tab and Grey pitched in for the tip, and I think he shorted the waitress on us. I went back and gave her five bucks and apologized. So it was about thirty dollars between Jason and me, and I finished up the last bit of my beer before we headed back up to the room to get ready and to have the car sent around to the front. While we were waiting downstairs in the lobby, Jason and I watched the parrots they keep there and the concierge told us that they were thirty years old. Jason had mentioned the bird to me once in the past and told me that one of his friends who was the bell captain here some years ago had his thumb nearly taken off by the old female.

Grey came down, finally, from his room and we all went out to the car, which had just been pulled around. The car was steaming inside with it's black exterior and windows up and the valet had kept the car running with the air conditioner at full blast. I tipped the valet and we all got in and started out of the resort. On our way out we passed between a row of about a hundred massive palms and looked back at the hotel as we made a right. It was an impressive façade to say the least, and then we were back in the middle of the desert, dusty, dry, and the road creating heat waves on the horizon. We followed side streets en route to Palm Springs and passed several very affluent communities and the upscale shopping district at El Paseo. There were many new buildings, obviously prospering in the quiet and eccentric wealth of Palm Desert. There were a couple of establishments that you don't see too often – a Goldman Sachs office, art brokers dealing in large sculpture and bronzes. And many of the world class shops that you'd be just as likely to run into on Florence, Michigan Ave, or Beverly Hills. But they were all built in the style of the desert – built white plaster with terra cotta tile roofs and Spanish or Italian blue tile accents. We continued past El Paseo and slightly downhill with the large distinctive desert mountains to our left.

We continued downhill, and then up and over the 10 freeway and down into Yucca Valley. It took us some time, but we were enjoying the drive. We needed to stop on our way through the park in the city of Joshua Tree for the gear, and also we stopped at a small grocery store off the main road before continuing though the park back down towards Palm Desert. There were a couple of worn out looking old men there smoking cigarettes and drinking beer out of cans wrapped in paper bags. Also there were a few San Bernardino county sheriffs. They were laughing and talking and pointing over towards the mountains.

I asked them if they ever saw anything interesting out there. One mentioned something about "Billy Boy," and they all start shaking their heads and chuckling to themselves in a proprietary, but polite way. David Grey tried to strike up a conversation with the sheriffs, his would-be comrades, but it did not go very well for him. They all had one-word responses. David Grey, pointing in different directions, asking about different parts of town and where there might be good things to do or see and the sheriff said, no, not so much around here.

I asked if any of them had ever been climbing on any mountains, and they all replied smiling that no, it was too much work, and what's the point of that anyway.

Just then an old timer with long, greasy, sun-bleached hair and a yellowish beard and clothes that looked hand made out of denim came walking over to us, acknowledging our presence. He was carrying what looked to be a bridle or some sort of leather strap for working with horses, sort of carrying it in both of his hands. He came up and asked us for some change. Jason offered him whatever was in his pocket and I didn't have any change on me. The old guy asked the locals and the sheriffs as well and they shouted him down and told him to beat it.
"What's wrong with the old timer" I said.
"He's a drunk."

I offered the sheriff a cigarette, which he took and nodded his head towards me once in approval.
"Where's he going?"

The sheriff spat out some of his chew.
"He sleeps out in the desert in the day time, especially if he can get drunk. Moves at night mostly. Eats trash."
"Do you ever have any problems out here? Any drugs?"
"Oh, they're out here."

Grey came back out from the store, still chewing something he must have just bought and consumed. With one hand he crumpled up and tossed the wrapper at the trashcan outside, but missed and then ignored the wrapper on the ground, letting it blow away. We all piled back into the car and started up the road towards the park. For several miles the scenery was much as it had been on our way into Yucca Valley; then, starting to wind around and climb into the dense patches of Yuccas and large rock piles, we were really in Joshua Tree. There were gigantic, round faces of granite and quartz mixed together and a few Joshua Trees. We rode further down thru sort of a valley and the road wound around through another yucca grove with some very large and impressive cactus varieties. We wound through some very nice organized camping areas with impressive rock formations and many campers, and then down a straightaway back towards the 10 freeway.

After several minutes we came out of the rock formations, and there were Joshua's lining both sides of the road, and we could see fields of sunflowers in the distance. I was up driving, Jason in the passenger seat, and we both glanced into the back seat. David Grey was passed out in the back. We shook out heads and smiled. Then the bottom dropped out on the valley and we drove down the alluvial fan, and you could see the power generating windmills, San Jacinto, and Palm Springs below. Now there were large mountains all around us. Gorgonio was to our right, and Jacinto ahead of us, and the road that stretched out below us.

We drove back into Palm Springs en route to Palm Desert on the other side of the valley, road winding finally down to the freeway. On our way back we passed the polo fields in Indio, the fences white against the green of the grass and the bright sun. We finally made it back to the Marriott.

The valet helped us with the goods we picked up at the mountaineering store. There was a crowd of people checking in, and the valet area was hot, and the trees and the water in the lobby were cool, and it was good to be out of the sun in the air-conditioned lobby. Our friend the concierge was glad to see us back and we shook hands. We all went to our rooms and got cleaned up and went down to the restaurant for lunch.

There are several restaurants in the Marriott, and they are all interconnected by a waterway of sorts, and boats deliver you to your place of choice. They hire attractive local high school or junior college kids to pilot these boats and accidents are very rare. But they have some really nice Italian and Japanese, and some passable Mexican food here. Along with your standard hotel café, which is where we ate lunch. David Grey was going on like he didn't like the food and didn't want to eat anything. So the waitress kept coming back and asking if she could help him and asking if he didn't like his food, etc. Grey had been acting funny since we meet in Palm Desert. He wasn't sure whether we knew that Kelley was with him down in La Quinta, and it made him rather nervous.
"Hm, well," I said, "Kelley and Jon are supposed to be here tonight."
"Actually I'm not so sure about that," Grey said.
"Why not?" Jason asked. "They'll be here."
"I'm pretty sure, actually, that they're going to flake out or be a little late," David Grey said.
He mentioned this in a very proprietary and superior way that pissed the both of us off.
"I'll put a hundred on them being here tonight," Jason said. I noticed that he was getting red.
"You're on," Grey said. "OK, Jack, you're our witness. One hundred dollars."
"I'll remember it," Jason said. I saw that he was really irritated now and I wanted to help things out just a bit.

"I'm sure they'll be here – could be tomorrow but they'll be here."

"Are you backing down?"

"Of course not, why would I? We can make it two hundred if you want to."

"I do and I will."

"Cut it out you guys," I said. "Or I'll want a couple of points for acting as your bookie."

"I'm just fine," Grey said and smiled. "I'm sure you won't miss the money."

"You haven't won it yet," Jason said.

We left the café to walk around the pools over to the bar to have a drink. Grey mentioned that he was going to go have his hair cut at the spa.

"Hey," Jason said to me, "do I have any chance of winning that bet?"

"Not so much. They're always late. If they're waiting for a wire or a direct deposit or something, they'll probably just come in tomorrow."

"I knew it before I took the bet. But I had to call him on his attitude. He's an OK guy, I guess, but who the hell is he? We invited Kelley and Jon in the first place."

I noticed Grey walking towards us across the way.

"Speaking of the devil."

"I hope he keeps a lid on his blue collar cop bullshit."

"The spa is being cleaned," Grey said, " It opens up in a couple of hours."

We had a beer at the poolside bar, sitting on slightly damp barstools looking out from the misted and cool patio to the large pool. After a while Jason went in to write some email and Great went back to the sap. It was still being cleaned, so he went up to his room and took a bath. I hung out by the pool and went for a walk. It was hot, but I stuck to all the shaded areas I could find and I walked through all of the little shops and had a nice time checking out the place again. I went to the front desk where I had some things delivered, including our concert tickets, so we were all taken care of in that regard.

A few women we're asking some questions at the concierge and one wandered over to where I was. She was wearing a skirt, bikini top, and bare feet.
"You were just at the pool, weren't you?"
"Yep."
"Oh, I thought I recognized you." So I smiled, nodded, and raised my eyebrows in sort of an understanding and thoughtful look. And I nodded and left.

I wanted to be left alone for a while, so I went back up to my room to sit down and think about some things. I went inside the room and it was cool and dark, with the curtains and shades covering any outside light. And the air was very dry when you breathed it in. I started to think about my friends and I kind of started talking to God, sort of like praying. I thought about Kelley and Jon and Jason and David Grey and myself, and all the musicians that were playing in the shows, separately for the ones I liked, and just thinking about the rest in general, and then I prayed for myself, and while I was sitting there with my head down and my hands folded in my lap I started to fall asleep, so I prayed a little longer that the show would be good, and that we'd have a great time and that we wouldn't have any accidents when we went climbing. I was thinking about some other things and then remembered that it would be really nice to have lots of money again, an so I prayed that I would find a great opportunity and be prepared when it came my way, and that I would hold onto the money when it came back to me, and thinking about money started me to thinking about Kevin and what he was doing and where he was living, regretting that I had left him that night at Mario's in downtown Riverside, and about something very personal Kelley had told me about him, and during this whole time I was thinking about how I must have looked at this moment, sitting here thinking and praying. I was embarrassed, being such a lousy Catholic as I was, but I realized that there really wasn't anything I was prepared to do about it, at least not now, and maybe not even later, but I thought about how great it would be as a social outlet and how prestigious and great the religion really is, and that I wish I could feel like a devoted and faithful person.

I wanted to have faith in something. Well, maybe next time I could; and then I was walking down towards the elevator and my nose was still stuffed up and my eyes were still all red. I made it outside and the sun was heavy and hot in the afternoon and I walked over to the bar and waited for the afternoon to cool down.

When we met for dinner we found that David Grey had made it to his spa appointment. His hair was cut and he probably had a manicure. He was visibly uncomfortable, and I didn't much feel like making him feel any better. If Kelley and Jon were coming, they would likely be arriving shortly. At about a quarter to nine, he announced that he was going to go out to the lobby to see if anyone has come in yet. I put my napkin on the table and told him that I'd keep him company. Jason said to hell with that I'm going to finish eating. He's like that with food. I told him that I'd be right back.

We walked over to the lobby, and I was enjoying Grey's impatience. I was hoping that Kelley would be waiting for us in the lobby. Up in the lobby, there was some activity but no Jon and no Kelley. By this time Grey was sweating and looking very nervous – more nervous that I think I have seen anyone and also impatient. So I was having a good time with it. David Grey had a tendency to bring out the best in everyone he meet. He really did.

In a couple of minutes there were several cars and taxis pulling up and guests arriving, each time a new group arrived we would get up and walk over to see if our friends were in the crowd. They did not show. We waited a little bit longer.

"I told you they weren't going to make it," David said. We were on our way back to dinner.

"I thought it would have been tonight," I said.

Jason was eating some dessert, which looked to be ice cream and there was a martini on the table as well.

"They didn't come, did they."

"Nope."

"Do you mind if I go to the ATM a little bit later for your two hundred?" Jason asked. "I haven't gone to the bank her yet."

"Let's just forget about it," Grey said. "Let's bet on something else."

The concierge came up to us with a folded piece of paper.

"It's for you." He gave me the paper.

The note said: "See you tomorrow."

"It's a note from our friends," I said.

I looked at the note much longer that I would have needed to -- just to read it. And I would have normally handed it over for everyone to read, but I just put it in my pocket.

"They're in Riverside for the night," I said. "They send their regards to the both of you."

I'm not sure why I felt like tormenting Grey so badly. Well, actually I do know why. I was insanely jealous about what he had happen to him. That I knew it was all going to happen didn't change how I felt about it, either. And the note came to me anyhow, so I didn't have to share it. It was the fact that David was acting like an ass, so false and confident, and proprietary about he and Kelley, and that made me hate him. So I pocketed the note without sharing it.

"Well," I said, "We'd better get ready to do some climbing. They can come out tomorrow night if they get here early enough."

"Sounds like a good idea," Grey said.

"The sooner the better."

"I'm easy, it's all good."

We sat in the café for a while and had some beer and then took a walk again out by the pool and looked out at the pool and all of the people waiting to get into the spa in the dark. I decided to have an early night. David and Jason stayed out and went to the nightclub. They must have been out pretty late because I wasn't awake to hear them come in.

The next morning I bought some coffees for the drive. We had decided to leave at nine o'clock in the morning. I was awake much earlier. I was sitting in the lobby reading the newspaper when I saw David Grey coming down across the way. He come up to me and sat down. "This is a great hotel," he said. "Did you have a good time last night, Jack?"

"Slept well."

"I didn't sleep at all. Jason and I were out late."

"Where did you guys go?"

"Just here. And after last call we went up to some sorority girls' room. Jason didn't tell you about it?"

"He's still sleeping."

"Yeah, he seems like a nice guy. I think he sleeps too much, though."

"Not when it counts, he doesn't." "Coffee – before the trip out to J-tree."

"Oh, yeah, about that. I don't think I'm going to join you guys today. You and Jason go ahead."

"What? I've already picked up your gear and everything."

"I'll pay you back for everything, really. You guys just go on ahead. I really should mention something, though. There might be some sort of miscommunication going on here about Kelley and Jon."

"Why," I said, "If they're stuck in Riverside having a good time, they may not be here for several days."

"Well that's just the thing," David said. "I think they wanted me to come out to Riverside to meet up with them, and then we'd all drive out together. I think that's why they're running late."

"What makes you think that?"

"Well, we've been emailing back and forth and we sort of agreed to it."

"Why in hell didn't you just stay in --," I was going to let him have it, but I stopped myself. I'm sure he would figure out what I was going to say, but that's just the thing. He's just the sort to guy not to have ever figured it our at all.

He was being proprietary again now and it was making him happy to be able to talk about he and Kelley out in the open. He enjoyed having me know that there was something between him and Kelley.

"Well, we're going to leave as soon as I can get Jason out of bed."

"I wish I could go along with you guys, I really do. And I know we've been looking forward to climbing all winter."

He was really pouring on the charm and it was disgusting. "But I really do need to wait for them here. As soon as they arrive, we'll join you guys."

"Let's go get Jason out of bed."

"See you at breakfast."

I found Jason up in his room. He was shaving.

"Oh yeah, he told me *all* about it last night," Jason said. "He's quite a little shit talker. He told me he spent two weeks with Kelley at La Quinta."

"That sonofabitch!"

"Whoa, whoa, don't get all pissed of just now. It's way too early in the trip. Hey, how did you ever get to be friends with this guy anyhow?"

"Don't remind me."

Jason looked around, in his towel and with half of his face shaved, the other half lathered and went on talking to his image in the mirror.

"Didn't you send me an email when I was in New York telling me about him? Hmmmm, it comes to mind that maybe you have some other cop buddies that you'd like to introduce me to?" He pulled his chin forward to reach the hairs on his neck. And started in shaving again."

"Oh yeah, you know some real winners as well."

"True, true but they all pale in comparison to this David Grey. Well it's strange because he can be a cool guy. I like him, but he's just such an ass."

"He is smart, and he is a talker."

"I know it. That's what I'm talking about."

We laughed.

"Yeah, go on and make light of the situation, but you didn't have to try to pick up girls with him last night at the bar."

"Was it terrible?"
"Oh as soon as he would come over, the girls would leave. I needed some backup. So what's the deal with him and Kelley, then? She *didn't*, did she?"
"Of course she did. They were at La Quinta together. As in *together* together."
"What a stupid thing to do. What in hell did she do that for?"
"She wanted to get away from it all, you know, the scene, and also she can't ever go anywhere by herself. Also, I think she thought that she might be helping him out or something."
"I can't believe the things that girls do. Why can't a girl ever help me out -- or something?" He looked at himself in the mirror. Washed his face clean of the lather and put some aftershave lotion on.
"My God, I'm getting old."
      He looked into the mirror again.
"As for David Grey," Jason said, "he bothers me, and he can go fuck himself and I'm glad that he's not going to be around for our climbing."
"Amen to that."
"We're going climbing. We're going climbing in Joshua Tree National park, and we're going to drink some beer and trip out on the fire and the rocks, and we're going to have ourselves some adventure."
"Let's get out of here," I said.

CHAPTER ELEVEN

It was hot outside in the valet area when we came down from the room with our bags and the things we would need for our climbing trip. People were in the lobby and some were getting into their cars. It was a busy day at the hotel. Jason got into the car and waited while I was in the gift shop buying soda and candy for the drive. When I got to the car, he had the air conditioning on full blast. I could barely sit on the leather seats with my shorts.

The valet stand is in the shade and still it really was very hot. David was in the driver's seat talking with Jason when I got to the car. When I tapped on the window they both opened their doors and David let me take the drivers seat.

David Grey walked backwards to the front of the hotel with his hands in his pockets waiting for us to leave. Our friend at the valet stand came over to us with some cold bottles of water for our trip and we tipped him for these. We were talking with the valet with our doors open and drinking some of the cold water when the car behind us sprang forward, screeched to a halt, and honked a loud horn. He had caught me off guard, and I spilled some of the water on myself. We all laughed but gave the impatient senior citizen bad looks. The valet looked on impatiently about this and went over to talk with the car behind us and the car honked again a second time which surprised Jason and I, and the valet became angry and we laughed. We decided to play with the guy and acted as if we were getting ready for our long drive, keeping our doors open. Jason was working on the CD changer in the trunk now and I was shifting items around in the back seat. I could hear the valet apologizing to the impatient driver and Jason and I had our laughs. The car behind us wanted us to leave. He laid on the horn for several seconds, and Jason and I shot the man some more bad looks and we were on our way. This we did only after we said a proper goodbye to our valet friend.

"Nice folks around here."

"Old people don't like their schedules interrupted," Jason said.

We started our trip in earnest at this point. We had a stack of good CDs, all of our climbing gear, and no Grey. So we were ready. The drive was nice and we decided that we'd take the scenic route through Palm Springs, and then stop there for lunch. We passed though the city of Palm Desert, and then down through Palm Springs again. We spotted a deli in old town Palm Springs that looked crowded and decided to stop there for lunch. There was a lively group of seniors at the bar, and we decided to sit there at the bar and talk, drink, and have some lunch.

Each of us had a beer, and cost four dollars with tax.

I put down five dollars, and intended to leave a one-dollar tip. But the lady brought back the dollar, thinking I

wanted the change back. We started talking with a couple of old timers who could have been our grandfathers. They eventually insisted on buying us a drink. They really enjoyed talking with us. And we enjoyed their company as well. Old people really know about life and it's interesting to hear that much of the stuff that goes on today went on back then, too. The words they use to describe women and relationships are different, and maybe folks didn't talk about everything so openly back then like they do now, but it doesn't change the fact that the same sorts of things were going on back then.
"So where are you fellas from?"
"Riverside."
"Oh, I have a such and such down there."
"Great, it's a good place to live."
"How long are you out here in Palm Springs?"
"We're just passing though on our way to Joshua Tree."
"In this heat?"
"Builds character."
"Have another drink?"
"All right," Jason said.
"We're out here for the big concert coming up."
"Oh yes, it's crowded just now, isn't it?"
"And what are you doing today?"
"We're going to go rock climbing out in Joshua tree for the next couple of days."
"You like climbing? What's the point? If you need to get somewhere, you can just walk or drive."
"Definitely. That's the point."
"Well, I hope you get to the top."
    We told everyone goodbye, and shook hands. The skin on their hands is very smooth and cold. I'm sure it is interesting for them to shake the hand of someone 60 years

younger and feel how hot and pliable and strong we are. How full of energy. It must be a small thrill. They had a good time talking with us, but the energy they had to expend to talk and drink with us made them tired, and I think that having a couple of beers with some young guys made their day, and that they were going to go home to bed after this.

Back in the car now, we climbed steadily out of the valley and into the mountains that you need to drive though to get down into Yucca Valley, and eventually into Joshua Tree. Looking back, we could see the desert and the windmills. There was no uniform horizon. There are some of the most rugged and extreme mountains all right here – San Gorgonio to our left, and San Jacinto behind us. We've been to the top of both, and wouldn't laugh at anyone else who has either. As we continued towards the park we came to the different looking rock formations of Joshua Tree that you didn't find anywhere else in the world. They weren't like the gray granite and forested mountains that you usually find. These were solid chunks of yellow dropped down right in the middle of the desert, many times sheer vertical slabs of granite, and other times a mix of granite and other stone. As we came up and around and through the pass, we could see the valley to the East.
"It's getting cold out here." It was probably 80 degrees.
"Yeah, pretty nice actually."
"We're getting up in altitude."
"Don't worry, we'll drop back down."

The road then dropped down and leveled off into a straight shot that ran through Yucca Valley and eventually into Joshua Tree, and then 29 Palms afterwards. There were houses along both sides of the road, and I'm not sure if all of them are still inhabited, and I remember reading

about folks coming out here to homestead the land, and getting it for free. And also I remembered that many of these people couldn't afford to get electricity or water to their houses. We turned into the park, and made it to the gate. The guard waved at us, and we stopped and showed him our pass.
"How are you guys?"
"Great. Going to do some climbing."
"Be safe, guys."
"Absolutely."

We continued up the street, past the strange houses, past the visitor center. The campground was packed, but there was a space for us and we parked and got out to stretch our legs. There wasn't anyone in the campsite next to ours.
"Good God. I hope it's a bit cooler tomorrow."

I started to set up the camp stove and cooler.
"Say, how much is that pass you have?"
"Sixty bucks for a year."
"How can you put a price on this kind of beauty?"
"The forest service regularly does so."
"Haven't they got anything cheaper? Like thirty bucks for a view of the Pacific Ocean?"

We were the only people around this part of the campground. Well, I thought, it's only a couple of days.
"Do you have beer in that cooler there?"
"Oh, yeah."
"Well that's all right then."

Jason was getting the tent set up and then throwing our bedstuffs and bags into the tent. I went back over to the table and did a survey of our food situation. We had the makings for stew, some good bread, plenty of beer, and some red wine. There were also a dozen eggs, a slab of bacon, and milk and coffee for breakfast. Jason was just finishing up with the tent, and it was getting on the afternoon. "Would you believe me if I told you I was getting cold out here?" he said. "I'm not too warm at all."

We put some warmer clothes on and decided to make some hot drinks with booze in them. In a few minutes the how water was ready on top of the camp stove and we had coffees with whiskey in it.

"Ah, this is my kind of place," said Jason. "It beats the hell out of home. Cold out here, but better than home."

We built a fire and prepared our stew in packets. We put the hamburger, potatoes, and carrots, several slices of onion, and salt and pepper in the fire and had a couple of beers to keep us busy while we were waiting for our dinner. When the stew was done and steaming, we finished off two bottles of the red wine along with the stew and it tasted good. I did a survey of the site and saw the many empty beer bottles and the empty bottles of wine. After dinner it was well into the evening and cold so we crawled into our sleeping bags to keep warm. The wind woke me up a couple of times. It was nice to be warm and in my sleeping bag.

CHAPTER TWELVE

I woke up early in the morning and took a look outside. I had to unzip the tent window, which pulled the tent in different directions. It was a pretty nice, clear, calm, day. Outside there were campers in their tents, some of the tents frayed from obvious use, and others were new-bought from REI. The particularly ragged tents belonged to people that were staying all week, not the folks out just for the weekend. A roadrunner ran by, hopped over a rock and then ducked through some chaparral. It stopped momentarily and looked quickly left, and right, and it reminded me of a lizard.

Jason was still sleeping, so I got ready, put my Reef sandals on and got out of the tent. There wasn't anyone else awake, so I went on a little walk. It was cool outside, and there were still some dew left from last night. I looked around for our wood to get a fire ready for breakfast. The sand was yellow and felt good underneath my feet. On the sandy gravel, I got the wood and newspapers ready for the fire. There were some bugs in the wood, and as I lifted the wood, they all ran away. Building the fire, I added three or four more logs and kept busy stoking it and making the fire even. Some lizards and birds nearby watched me make the fire.

When I took a peek back in the tent, I saw that Jason was still sleeping. I was hungry, so I continued to prepare the breakfast by putting coffee on the fire. Now Jason woke up and started sniffing and I could tell he was coming out of the tent.

"Good morning there -- saw you hard at work and I didn't want to interrupt you. What were you doing, there buddy? Having fun?"

"You lazy bastard!"

"Showing great respect and admiration, I see? And so early in the morning. Excellent. We'll have to keep that up every day we're out here."

"Get the hell out of bed," I said.

"What? I never get up."

He crawled back beneath all of the sleeping bags and blankets.

"Just try and talk me into getting up."

I went on having breakfast and started to get our climbing gear ready. I flaked out several ropes, and put together a couple of generously appointed racks of protection for our climb.

"Aren't you going to ask," Jason asked.

"I'm going to eat."

"Food? You didn't mention food. I thought that this getting up business was all an academic exercise. Go ahead and keep at that fire, and I'll be right out."

"Go to hell."

"Respect and admiration, that's the ticket," Jason said as he put some shorts on.

"Show some respect."

I started out of the site with my ropes and racks of gear slung around my neck.

"Whoa, where are you going?"

I walked over and poked my head in the tent again to see what he was doing.

"Aren't you going to show some respect and admiration?" I flipped him off.

"That's not respect nor admiration," he said.

As I was walking around the site, I head Jason singing in a high falsetto.

"I don't practice Santeria – I ain't got no crystal ball. If I had a million dollars well I'd, I'd spend it all … and that Pancho that she found …."

He kept up with the high falsetto until he emerged from the tent. By that time I had stowed our climbing gear and was sitting at a table reading a week old Press Enterprise.

"What's this respect and admiration thing?"

"What this? Don't you know about respect and admiration?"

"No? Who brought this up?"

"It's quite the rage in L.A. Just like horn rimmed sunglasses."

The food was ready, and consisted of eggs, bacon, and toast. Or burnt bread, rather, with butter.

"Ask the waitress if she can't bring some jam over, would you, and please show some admiration."

"Haven't you got any?"

"That's not respect. I wish I could speak Japanese. It's the language of respect."

The coffee tasted good and we drank it out of a couple of stone mugs I had brought. I was able to find some strawberry jam out of little glass jars from Knott's Berry Farm.

"Thanks."

"Hey, that's what I'm talking about. Show some respect. You have to use lots of long words and don't forget to mention the Four Seasons hotel and try to throw in something literary."

"I could ask what sort of jam we'll get into today up on the rock."

"Indeed."

"OK, I've got something literary to say. David Grey."

"Now you're talking. Now why is David Grey literary, and please show some respect."

Jason downed his coffee and poured himself more from the pot.

"Sonofabitch. It's way too early in the morning."

"OK, now. And you claim that you want to be a writer, too? You're just a computer programmer. A disillusioned burnt out computer programmer living in the 909. You should show admiration for all things immediately after you wake up each morning, with literary style and thought just waiting to come out of your mouth, and you really should be living in LA."

"Where did you hear all of this from?"

"It's all over the place. Are you kidding? I read it in the papers, hear it one the radio, people tell it to me on the telephone. Do you ever get out when you're in Riverside? Do you see anyone? Talk to anyone? Do you even have a telephone number you can be reached at?"

"Drink your coffee," I said.

"Caffeine is a good thing. It helps a woman do his thing and a man be at her best. You know what your problem is? You live in the 909. You're one of the worst kind of people there, too. Nobody that lives in the 909 ever wrote anything worth printing. Not even for the papers."

He sipped at his coffee.

"You're a 909er, you've lost touch with the world. You get crazy, silly, funny living out here. Living out here in the dirt and with the meth labs has spoiled your reality. You're an alcoholic and you're obsessed with women and sex. All you do is sit in these cafes, not doing any work. You drink in your bars. You sit in your cafes. You ride motorcycles, and you drive a truck. You are a 909er, see?"

"Sounds like the life to me," I said. "What about work?"

"Work? I've never seen you do any work. Do you ever work?"

"Some folks say that your women take care of you, other say it's impossible because you can't get hard and that you really do actually work for a living…"

"No, I was just at the wrong place at the wrong time."

"Things like that between men can't ever be said, they can only be felt. Use it to your advantage. Use the old mysterious bit – sort of like Magic and his balls. That's right, his magic balls – not too sure about those balls these days, now I wonder how many times he's used that line himself. Now Shaq on the other hand … "

He kept going and going for a good bit, but he stopped. I think he may have gotten self-conscious about the crack he made about impotence, but I wanted to get him going again because he was as always, a very, very funny man.

"It wasn't his balls," I said, "it was his women."

"I heard it was his boys."

"Well some women are sort of like boys, you can use them the same way."

"But you don't use magic on them."

"No, you use your Johnson."
"OK, let's forget about all that."
"Suits me fine, I was just standing up for Magic's balls."
"I think he was fine at handling his balls. And I think you're a fine, fine man Jack Baker. Anyone ever tell you that?"
"Hey, you're a fine, fine, man and I like you more than anyone alive. And you know I couldn't say that back in LA, it would mean I'm a homo or something. There's nothing wrong with that, of course. You know, that's what the war in Iraq was all about. George Bush was in love with Saddam Hussein, and Bush just went to war over a lovers spat. It's all about sex."
He stopped.
"You want to hear some more of this stuff?"
"Go for it," I said.
"Oh man, I'm so done. How about at lunchtime."
"Jason, man."
"You bastard."

    We packed up some food for lunch and packed our climbing gear, and we both put our packs on. I carried two ropes and two racks of climbing gear slung over my neck. We started off on a sand trail, and then went across a clearing that crossed some Joshua Tree groves and crossed that and went down and around a slope and some large boulders. We shuffled down and around more boulders. The rocks were cool from the evening. We could hear other campers stirring now down below, talking in the morning. The path now crossed several washes, and there were some old wooden fences that were probably once a place for people to tie their horses up on. In the sandy wash, we shuffled through the sand for a bit before reaching more solid footing up on the bank of the wash. It was hard to notice, but we were steadily climbing, and we looked back to see the tents, all different colors, the sandy trail, and the green of the cactus and vegetation. We arrived at the base of the rock tower we had planned to climb. It was several hundred feet straight up, with some good exposure, and with an overhanging rappel off the back to finish. It was one of the best climbs in Joshua Tree.

"Some nice desert here," Jason said.

We approached the rock through campsite #91 and made our way around to the south face. I shook off all of my gear, laying everything out on the ground so I could see it well, and made a final survey of the climb. There weren't any bolts on our chosen route to my knowledge, and we'd have to place and clean only naturally anchored protection on our way up. I was going to lead the climb and so we set up the first belay for Jason down at the bottom using two runners equalized to a couple of opposed locking 'biners. Each of us tied our figure eights and put our climbing shoes on. After I had double-checked my own harness, we came together and I checked to see that Jason's harness was tied correctly, the belt passing through and back over the buckle. The act of roping together is an intimate one, and it's your own life, see? So I gave his harness a strong tug by his figure eight and he did the same thing to mine. I started out climbing up the first pitch, getting my legs and feeling myself out a bit.

"On belay?"

"Belay on. How are you feeling?" Jason asked.

"It's a good day to die. Climbing." I responded.

"Climb on."

The climb started out on a vertical seam, a couple inches deep. I could get two fingers in at a time and my feet were placing very well and I moved up to a right-

leaning crack, which could accommodate my clenched fist. I was able to bury my whole hand in the crack, and clinch my fist so that my weight wouldn't pull it out and I reached with my right hand and pulled a camming device off of my rack. I placed the cam in the crack, and pulled the rope through the gate of the carabineer. I decided to place another friend on this right leaning crack because it ran up a sort of overhanging roof and if I were to take a fall at this point, it wouldn't be pretty. So I placed another friend.
"ON BELAY?"
"BELAY ON!"
"CLIMBING!"

The next couple of moves went fast and ended with my left foot wedged in the right leaning crack and my body over the top of the roof. There was some stable, smooth rock that didn't give me too much trouble for the next several meters. I wanted to make my way over to the right side of the south face, so I traversed over a bit, smearing the stone, to a place that looked like it would make a good anchor for Jason's belay up. I started to work quickly on getting his anchor set up. I found a very nice two-inch ledge to stand on and I did all of my work standing up. I placed two cams and a chalk in the crack and equalized it all with a bandoleer, clipped in, and took a couple of quick breaths.
"OFF BELAY."
"BELAY OFF."

Jason was out of sight but we could hear each other's climbing commands well. It took him several minutes to clean the anchor.
"UP ROPE."

I started hauling the rope, which came up through the protection I had left on the right leaning crack and roof,

and over to my belay station. At one point the rope was stuck in the crack, but between Jason and myself, we were able to whip it free without too much trouble. When I felt the rope get tight I let out some slack.
"UP SLACK!"

He wanted it tight, so I pulled in the slack and gave him some security on the belay. He was climbing fast, and well, and he made it up to the roof and I could tell he was cleaning the protection.
"UP SLACK!"

I could hear confidence in his voice. It was a good sign. The roof was really a 5.10a with some exposure and possibly an R rating, so I took out as much slack as I possibly could during his move over the overhang. I'm not sure if he knew exactly what he had signed up for on this climb, so I was sort of laughing about the move he had just made when he traversed over and settled down on the ledge where I was belaying him.

"You sonofabitch, Baker," Jason said between breaths.
"How are you feeling?" I grimaced.
"Good climb. Want to let me lead this next pitch?"
"Go for it." That was a good sign, too.

Since he was leading the next pitch, we could keep our gear much as it was, with the exception of that I had to make sure the protection was equalized and balanced to handle and upward force rather than a downward force. The protection was fine, and we both agreed, and so he got ready to lead the second pitch of the climb. Jason had the gear he had cleaned from the belay station at the bottom, and also the gear that he cleaned from the right leaning crack, and I handed him the rest of my rack, which he shouldered. We issued our climbing commands quietly to underscore their importance.

"On belay?"
"Belay is on."
"Climbing."
"Climb."

He started up the second pitch, straight up the south face of the rock and I knew this was the crux of the climb. He was working hard and fast, and his breathing was good. His legs looked all right as well, and his moves were confident. He was out of sight in a couple of minutes, and I was letting out my belay steadily. The exposure was good on this climb, and I know it's why he wasn't joking or talking. On other easier climbs, we could joke around, but not today.

There was a ledge at the top of the south face, which Jason must have made it up to, because he didn't need any more rope. I had given Jason plenty of slack on this pitch, paying it out as it was taken up little by little. And so the rope wasn't being taken up any more, and I knew that he had reached the ledge and was probably working on his anchor and belay station. The wind was blowing lightly and my sweat dried right away and gave a cool sensation. Looking down, there were some people gathering to watch our ascent. I was eager to start climbing.

"ON BELAY?"
"NO!"

I knew the placement was a bitch up there on the ledge so I tried to rest my legs, alternately locking my knees back.

"OK!" Jason called.

I could hear the rope being brought up and it didn't snag on anything, so finally when he had it all hauled in, I was able to start to work.

"ON BELAY?"
"BELAY ON."

I made pretty quick work of the belay anchor, but the chalk was in there pretty good, as usual, and I had to use my tool to tap it out. I put the cams on my rack, and strung the extra webbing around my neck and secured it all so it wouldn't catch on the rock as I was climbing.

"CLIMBING!"
"CLIMB ON!"

The south face was nice, and the sun was getting hot. It was real work getting up the smooth face, using my fingertips to hold myself up on the rock. The shoes were performing well, and the rock was in the direct sun, which heated the soft rubber on the soles and made them stick to the granite face. I continued up the face and was making good progress. Jason was keeping the rope tight, which suited me fine, and I made it up to the ledge and sat down next to catch my breath. I led the last pitch so we could keep the belay on, and pulling myself up the final few feet, I flipped around and sat on the peak for a couple of seconds to admire the view alone. There was a crowd down there, watching us, and I could see a couple of them clapping. This wasn't El Capitan, but the view of the desert was spectacular. There were a couple of bolts at the top which I clipped into and made very quick work of a final belay station for Jason and he made it up to the peak and we congratulated each other on making the climb in such good form. He rappelled down first, as it the custom. The first man to reach the peak leaves last, and I had a very good time rappelling down the 150ft overhang down into the invisible, shady depths below.

Down at the bottom we shared a couple of laughs from the exhilaration of the climb and made our way back

to the campsite, which fortunately had some good shade from the tall rocks it was situated beneath. There was plenty of cold beer in the cooler, and after we each had several, Jason went back into the cooler for some more. He came back over to his chair, drying his hands on his shorts, with two more cold bottles of beer.
"Give this a try," he said, snapping the cap off the bottle.
"Let's try this."
The beer was cold, refreshing, and a bit skunky.
"That's not terrible, that beer there," Jason said.
"It's good and cold."

We started in on our lunch, which was dry salami, several tomatoes, and some cheese that we shared and cut with a large Swiss Army Knife that my sister had picked up for me in Luzanne last winter.
"Salami."
"There's some bread in the car."
"Did you find the mustard?"
"Can't eat French mustard, it's anti-patriotic."
"The French are all anti-patriotic, you know."
"Yes, indeed."

Jason set down the salami and picked up the mustard.
"People of the United States of America – we can no longer allow this symbol of French anti-patriotism to bear the name of the country that harbors terrorists and that hides weapons of mass destruction, as evidenced here in exhibit one. Plain yellow mustard."
"Let's have another beer."
"You're drunk."
"On beer?"
"Sure."

"It's just the heat," Jason said. "They ought to do something about this damn heat out here."
"Have another beer."
"We only have the case."
"Do you know what you are?" Jason looked at the bottle.
"No," I said.
"You're the product of the cosmological universe - molecular matter, I constructed you, fuck you –"
"You are drunk!"
"On beer?"
"Yes, on beer."
"Well, maybe I am."
"Want to take a nap?"
"Sure."

We moved the handles on the chairs so that the backs lay down into the sand, and they were really only just pads, and we looked up at the shady cool rocks.
"Are you sleeping?"
"No," Jason said. "Just thinking."

I closed my eyes. It was nice laying in the shade on the sand.
"Hey," Jason said, "what about this Kelley deal?"
"What about her?"
"Are you in love with her?"
"Yeah."
"How long?"
"For a hell of a long time now."
"Jesus!" Jason said. "I'm sorry, man."
"It's all right, " I said. "I don't give a rats ass anymore."
"Are you sure about that?"
"I'm sure. I'm also sure that I really, really don't want to talk about it."
"Are you pissed at me for asking?"

"Why should I be?"

"I'm going to pass out," Jason said. He took his shirt off and threw it over his face.

"Hey, Jack," he said, "Aren't you Catholic?"

"Yeah."

"What does that mean to you?"

"I'm not sure."

"OK, I'm going to sleep, stop talking so much."

I fell asleep, too. When my eyes opened up Jason was cleaning up and packing the lunch away. I pulled myself off the ground and started on the beer bottles that were thrown around the campsite. It started to get dark and we needed to put some warmer clothes on and start a fire.

We stayed in Joshua Tree National Park for five days and had some good climbing. It was cold at night, and the days were hot. There was enough of a breeze blowing to keep cool in the shade. We drank and talked with a British guy named Wright that we met in a bar, who was out here from Redondo Beach. He was a good guy and he went on two climbs with us. We didn't hear anything from David Grey nor from Kelley or Jon.

CHAPTER THIRTEEN

We woke up early and decided to go into town for breakfast again at the Internet Cafe in the city of Joshua Tree. Brett Wright was there again over his newspapers.
"All right then," he said, "Can't seem to stay away from the email, can you then, mate?"

I took my place at the terminal and the waitress arrived with a hot cup of coffee for me. Brett was back to his newspaper. I opened up an email dated Monday:

THE 909

```
Date: Mon, 8 May 1999 10:57:14 -0800
From: Jonathan Boswell <jonboswell@909thebook.com>
To: Jack Baker <jackbaker@909thebook.com>
Subject: RE: this weekend
```

Dear Jack,

We arrived at the Marriott on Sunday, and had a big party. Kelley especially had too much of a good time and I thought that it would be a good idea to get her away from the party, so we're over here in La Quinta staying at the resort for a couple of days. We're going to leave here on Tuesday night and will be back in Palm Desert for Wednesday. We're really sorry to miss out on things in Joshua Tree, and I'm sure Kelley will be recovered by Tuesday and actually she's feeling better as we speak. You'd think that I would have known better than to leave her alone – We've gone through all of this before, but it's not easy to keep such good track of her. You understand.

Take care,

Jon

"What is today, Tuesday?" I asked Wright.
"It's Wednesday, mate. Yes, indeed, yes, it is. Wednesday it is. Easy to forget out here."
"We've been out here a week."
"Well I hope you're not thinking of jumping ship just yet mate."
"We're going to have to leave this afternoon."
"Oh, that's not in the spirit mate. I was hoping to take another walk around the park."
"We're meeting our friends in Palm Desert."

"Well we do what we have to, don't we? Yes, indeed we do, yes, yes. Indeed. Well we did have a time then didn't we, mate?"
"Why don't you come over to Palm Desert, it's not that far away. We're going to have some big parties, and we can drink and look at girls."
"Yes, I'd like to very much mate, but my holiday is quite at it's end here, and I should like to do some more climbing before I return to the trouble and strife."
"You want all of the glory for yourself, don't you?"
"Well I say, yes indeed. Yes I do mate."
"Well I'd love to get some of that as well you know."
"Come on mate, be a good Yank and stay on another day."
"We really have to get going," I said.
"Shame, really."

After we ate our huge breakfast of eggs and toast, Jason and I sat out in front of the café warming ourselves in the sun. We talked things over and I thought I'd go back in and check my email one more time before we made our way back to break camp. There was a note from David Grey and it only read, "I'll be there Thursday."

I motioned for Jason to come over and read the mail.
"What party is he going to?"
"What an informative communication." I said.
"Let's get back to the desert. No need to make Kelley and Jon make the drive all the way out here for nothing."
"Are you going to reply to him?"
"Let's not stoop to his level."
"What are you going to write him?" Jason asked.
" ` Be there today `, and that's it."

I sent the message to Grey and we made our way to the car. On our way back to the park we saw Wright's car

THE 909

at the visitor center so we stopped to talk with him one last time before we left.

"Nice little museum they've got here," Wright said. We met him as he was coming out. "I'm not a big museum man, myself. No, I'm not -- no."

"I'm not big on museums either," Jason said.

"It is quite a tribute to the living desert, though," Wright said. "I've been telling myself to take a peek every day now."

"It's just not as much fun as climbing, now then, is it?"

"Indeed not, no. No it isn't mate."

We were standing in the small parking lot outside of the visitor center.

"Wasn't that a pub back down the way?"

"It looked sort of like a pub to me." I said.

"How about a couple of pints, then?"

We all went back to the bar and drank a pitcher of beer each. Brett wouldn't let us chip in on the tab. I asked the waitress to take my card, but Wright had her convinced not to take any of our money.

"It won't be any time soon that I'll have as much of a time than we had here this week, mate."

"We had a great time Brett."

"Really, mate, it was such a time and I thank you."

"We'll climb together some time soon. Send me an email. We'll put together a trip."

"Indeed mate, we must. We had quite a time."

"How about one more pitcher between us?"

"Excellent idea my man," said Wright.

"I've got this round," said Jason. "Or we don't have it at all."

"Oh, come on mate, you know it's my pleasure."

"This one is on me. It's my pleasure."

The waitress brought over the fourth pitcher, and we used the same glasses to pour it all around. Brett lifted his glass.

"Cheers mates. Good times as you yanks say."

Jason laughed and gave Brett a slap on the back.

"Brett mate."

"You yanks don't use words like mate, now don't you mate?"

"We can use worlds like that since we're friends," Jason said.

"Baker, mate, we've had quite a time haven't we?"

"Yes, let's have some more of that pitcher," I said.

"Seriously mate, seriously. I haven't had such a good time."

We walked back to our cars from the bar with Wright between the two of us. We stopped in at the Thai place and Brett gave us both his business card and gave us his home address and telephone for his place at the beach.

We got into our car and Brett stood behind us and waved as we started off. We could see him in the rear view mirror still waving at us as we headed off to break camp.

"That's a good guy," Jason said.

"He did have a good time, didn't he?"

"Wright? Absolutely."

"He should have come on with us to the desert."

"I think he wanted to do some solo climbing."

"Yeah. Well that's a good point, and also you can never tell how he would have gotten along with everyone."

"I guess not."

We arrived in Palm Desert late in the day and we stopped our car as close as we could get to the main valet area. People were coming in car after car, checking in for the concert. There were even several police cars, which you never see around here. Tina Bold was drinking a beer out of the bottle in the lobby.

"Your friends are already here," she said.

"Jon Boswell?"

"That's right. And Kelley and David Grey."

Tina raised her eyebrows and smiled when she mentioned the latter names as if she was in on a secret that Jason and I didn't know about.

"What time did they get in?"

"Last night. Are you guys in the same rooms?"

"Yes, same as before we left."

"Where are our good friends right now?"

"I think they're at the pool bar."

"How's the crowd shaping up for the show?"

"Well it's the crowd you'd expect. A bunch of trendy kids coming into to see a pop show."

"Yes, they've never seen real punk rock before. Have you seen Souxsie around?"

I smiled. We shook hands and I pulled her in closer so that I could give her a hug.

"See you around."

She smiled, raised her eyebrows, and gave me a nod. Every time we talked it was as if music was a special secret between us; a very shocking but really very deep secret that just us knew about. She always reacted as if this secret would disgust outsiders, something antisocial, but it was something that the two of us could understand. It just wouldn't be good to tell this secret to someone who just couldn't understand.

"Your friend Jason, he's into the scene as well isn't he?"

"Yes, he came all the way from San Francisco for this show."

"Really." Tina shrugged, frowned, and nodded in disbelief. "But he's not punk like we are, is he?"

Being punk is a state of mind. It's passion for anti-establishment and going against the norm. A punk is someone who is passionate about life and passionate about music that expresses these types of feelings. Tina Bold has hosted a radio show in Riverside for more than ten years, promoting punk rock music, and under her attractive and gregarious skin lays a true punk. You will see her at many of the areas shows. We often talked about music and punk rock and what makes someone a real punk. I have been coming to the Coachella festival since it started a couple of years ago and it was very nice to meet up with Tina and to talk with her about what each of us felt about punk music. And to meet and talk to the artists and performers involved with the concert. These people are all true punks.

Tina has the special quality of being a person that can forgive anyone for any digression so long as they were a true music fan. She could forgive them flaking on her show, cursing on their album and getting her suspended from the radio by the FCC. She forgave me for having trendy, preppy friends. With her ever mentioning it to me, I knew that my friends didn't impress her and it was a small embarrassment between to two of us. Sort of like a stage diver at a concert that does not get caught by the crowd.

Jason had gone upstairs to our room and I found him washing up and changing his clothes.
"What's new with DJ Tina?"
"She was telling me about some of the bands that are checking in tonight."
"Let's find the group and go down there."
"Alright. They're probably at the pool bar."
"Have you got the tickets for the shows?"

"Yes, and I have them for all of the other shows as well."
"What is she like?"

He was shaving, which he did about once a week, and was going against the grain to get all of this little hairs that sometimes grow to look like stubble.

"She's a cool chick. Not attracted to me, I can tell you, but very smart."
"Did you ever get together with her?"
"She's always had a significant other."
"Must be swell to be bisexual."

We got into the elevator and punched the lower level button to take us down to the pool. There were several closed hotel shops. I scanned the crowd of tables for Kelley and Jon. And finally spotted them. Kelley and Jon and David Grey. Kelley and Jon were well-tanned and wearing very fashionable Gucci sunglasses with tinted lenses, and black swim trunks. David Grey was sort of white, sunburned, and squint eyed and he was wearing blue jeans. Kelley noticed us walking over the bridge to the pool area and she waved us over to their table. She flipped her hair at us when we got to the table.

"Hey you guys!" she shouted at us.

Kelley was radiant. Jon was a good guy and had an intense, affable character that made people feel comfortable and happy. Jon stood up and shook my hands, using both hands, which felt nice. We shook because we were happy to see one another. David Grey didn't stand up and I think he shook our hands because he simply could not avoid it.

"Where in the world have you been?" I asked.
"I just brought the group over last night," Grey said.
"That's a bunch of crap," Kelley said. "We would have been a long time ago if you hadn't come along."
"You would never have found the place."

"Bull shit! Hey, you guys are tan. Look at you Jason."

"Did you guys have any good climbs?" Jon asked. "We wish we could have seen you guys."

"Not bad at all. Good weather and some serious exposure."

"Any interesting people out there?"

"We met a couple of Brits – one named Wright – ever know him Jon? He was a hacker once upon a time."

"What a guy," Join said. "Those were the days. Oh, I wish the good old days of computer hacking were back."

"Oh, shit."

"You were a hacker, Jon?"

"Was I?"

"He was the best hacker in the world," Kelley said. "Tell them about the time you took over Domino's pizza."

"I will not. I've told you that story before."

"You never told me that story," David Grey said.

"I can't tell that story. That story is a discredit to my character."

"Tell them about the time you took over that cellular network."

"I can't tell that story. That story is a discredit to my mother."

"What are you guys talking about?"

"Kelley will tell you all about it."

"Go ahead Kelley, tell us."

"You want me to tell you about computer hacking?"

"You must have broken into at least one computer in your career…"

"Well, yes, that I have. I guess I have. I will tell you about the time that we took over the Domino's pizza in Beverly Hills. We had their telephone lines routed to our hotel room in Vegas. The instant we initiated the forward on the local switch, calls started coming in. So at first we started out with things like, 'Thank you for calling Dominoes pizza – can I interest you in our rat meat special?"

Everyone laughed.

"And then Jon started to get mean," Kelley said.

"So after a while we started taking calls from all sorts of folks and we mentioned to several women that maybe she should get off their fat asses and walk down and get their own pizzas. We knew that these comments went over well in their households when we started getting calls from irate husbands – they would ask us to put the manager on the line so I would hand the phone over to Jack here and he would give them a piece of his mind as well. 'Yeah, you too mister, why don't you come on down here and I'll kick your ass, and bring your fat wife, too, I'll kick her ass too!" Everyone was laughing at this.

"Yeah, I know, it wasn't very nice. But we sure got a good hearty laugh out of it. I really do feel sorry for the manager that night. I'm sure several of the people we talked to went down to the location to find the staff relaxing, laughing, and having a good time since no calls were coming in. Just imagine that scene. Well, there you have it. I was quite the hacker in my day."

"Tell us more about the phones, Jon," Kelley said.

"You didn't think the Dominoes story was funny enough?" Jon asked. We were all still rolling on the floor. "It really was pretty funny. In any case, so we kept up with the gag, taking orders for pizzas and offending the good clientele of Beverly Hills. I'm sure the manager caught some serious hell when we let him have his phones back." John waited a couple of seconds. "Too bad, so sad for that guy," he said.

"You don't really feel sorry for him, do you Jon?" Kelley.

"Well," Jon smiled.

"How did you end up in jail?" Jason asked.

"Arrested suddenly, then sentenced gradually."
"What finally sent you away?"
"People who talk. Hackers. Friends. Enemies."
"Tell them about your final sentence hearing," Kelley said.
"It's all a blur. It was so long ago I can barely remember. The CTO of AT&T came to testify on my behalf."
"Tell them what you did to the FBI."
"I can't tell anyone about that or I'll go back to jail. Hey, are we going to go see that band now, or what?"
"Let's go."

  I waived the waiter back over to our table, signed to my room, and we all started to make our way over to the venue. I was walking next to Kelley and Grey caught up with us and came up over on her side. The three of us continued up and around the sidewalk across from the golf course and towards the pool area where they had the stage set up.

  Some locals had set up and were selling beer in cans for $1.00 a piece.
"This is where we'll come when we're strapped for cash," Kelley said and smiled at the guys.

  One of the guys tapped his buddy on the shoulder to take a look at Kelley. They were all staring at her, and followed her with their eyes when she had passed.

  At the gate to the concert area a bouncer took our tickets as we went in. We walked through the gate and got our hands stamped. There was a small stage and speakers set up with a soundman towards the rear of the area. A pit was forming right in front of the stage, people pushing their way to the front to be right there with the band. The band had four pieces. There were the drums, with a couple of pillows stuffed into the bass drum's cavity. The DJ, who had what look to be a single turn table and mixer setup, and

THE 909

a microphone. The bass player. The rhythm guitarist, who was wearing a t-shirt that said "ARMY" on it and had what looked like an iron on of the bust of a German shepherd. The lead singer also had a guitar and he was wearing a tight t-shirt with the sleeves cut off. I think they were from Nebraska or something and had started to make it in the L.A. scene.

We walked over to a short wall towards the right hand side, facing the state. We all climbed up and sat on the wall to watch the show.

"Check that out," I said.

On the other side of the artificial lake you could see the night sky loaded with stars and people were gathering on the other side of the lake to watch the show. People were also sitting on their balconies to look and see what was going on down below.

"They must thing something's going on here," Kelley said.

"They want to see the band."

Jon and Jason weren't on the wall, but down below milling around with the crowd. They waved at us and shouted hello.

"When are they going to get started," Grey said.

The band was tuning up and it looked like the DJ had some issues with the sound guy and he kept pointing to his turntable and mixer. The sound guy would shrug his shoulders and the DJ would shake his head and keep pointing frantically to the turntable and then to the mixer. The lead singer shook his head and smiled, I think right at Kelley.

"They don't look very professional," Kelley said.

The lead singer struck a strong, distorted chord on his guitar and all of the people in front of us stood up and suddenly our great view disappeared. I stood up on the wall and took Kelley's hand and pulled her up with me. The bass player started in before the drummer and way laying down a thick line. The drummer came in slowly at this point, too, and the lead singer and guitarist started to move around the stage. He was letting things build up a bit, sort of walking and dancing subtly around the stage gauging the crowd and the pit. He was making eye contact with the other guitarist, the bassist, and the drummer, smiling and sort of laughing and you could tell there was some inside joke or knowledge that only they understood.

The lead started jumping up and down quickly with the beat and after four counts he and the rhythm guitarist started in on their pre-chorus.
"Wow, these guys are good, aren't they?" Kelley said. We had a good view of the stage.
"Look how the lead signals to the other guys," I said. They've practiced this before.
"You think so?"
"Just watch."
"They're playing so fast."
"Check it out, he'll show the drummer when he wants to break out of the last chorus."

The crowd started to move around quickly, especially just in front of the stage. Someone climbed up on the stage and dove off into the front section, and the crowd was just a bit too thin and only supported him for several seconds before he sort of tumbled down to the ground. All we could see were his tennis shoes in the air for the instant before he disappeared into the melee. A large bouncer dove into the crowd and pulled and grabbed the guy and yanked him out of the crowd to kick him out of the show. Several people in the crowd gave the bouncer a hard time and the band make some remarks about leaving us

THE 909

alone. This didn't make the bouncer very happy and he kicked the kid out of the show any way. Rules were rules. The band played several more songs, good melodies and driving rhythms, and we caught sight of the guy that had gotten kicked out of the show trying to sneak back in. We had left our wall and were wandering around the back of the venue listening to the next band when we spotted Jason and Jon over at the pool bar.

"Pretty amazing band," Kelley said.

"Was the last band as good as the first one?" David Grey asked. "The crowd seemed to quiet down a bit after they went off."

"What do you mean good?" Jason asked. "They all sing better than I do."

"They only play this well when they're on stage. Listen to them at home and they're just as good as you are in the shower."

"Yeah right," Jason said, "Don't you ever try to listen to me in the shower, Jon."

"Word," Jon said, "those were some pretty decent bands – did you see those stage divers?"

"Uh, yeah," Kelley said. "I had no idea they would do that here."

"Did you see everybody boo the bouncer?"

"Must suck being a bouncer," David Grey said.

"Oh really?" Jon said. "Seems like you'd actually make a pretty decent bouncer yourself, David."

"I'm not sure I know what you mean, Jon."

"Bouncers are always such meatheads. They don't make anyone happy and they're always hanging around all the time."

We were all uncomfortable. Jason coughed and laughed. David Grey was mad. Jon went on with his talking.
"Seriously, I would think you'd be the perfect bouncer. You'd never have to say anything, either. Those guys don't ever talk, do they? Go ahead and say something. Don't just sit there with your arms crossed like that"
"I just mentioned something, Jon. About the bouncer."
"What else do you have to say? Come on now, we're all having a good time."
"Give it a rest, Jon, you're hammered," Kelley said.
"I'm not hammered, I'm serious. Is David Grey going to go after Kelley all the time like a goddamned bouncer after a kid just trying to have some fun?"
"Shut your mouth Jon and try to have some class."
"Screw class. Who has any class really anyhow except for the band? Wasn't that band good? Didn't you like them Jason? Come on, spit it out David. Don't just stand there all pissed off. So what if you did have sex with Kelley? She's been with much better men than you."
"Shut up," Grey said. He got up. "Shut up, Jon."
"Don't you stand up there and act like you're going to put the beat down on me. That wouldn't hurt me. David, tell me. Why do you chase Kelley around like that meathead bouncer? Don't you know nobody wants you? I know when nobody wants me around. Why don't you know when nobody wants you around? You followed us to La Quinta where nobody wanted you, and followed Kelley around like a dirty bouncer. You know I'm right, don't you?"
"Shut the hell up, you're drunk."
"Maybe I am drunk – aren't you? Why don't you ever drink, Grey? You didn't have a good time at La Quinta

because nobody wanted you around at their table. Well you have to agree with them, don't you? I agree with them. Talk to me Grey, don't you agree?"
"Fuck off, Jon."
"I agree with all of them. Don't you agree with them? Why do you chase Kelley around? Don't you understand? How in the hell do you think it looks to *me*?"
"You're quite the person to talk about understanding," Kelley said.
"You understand everything."
"Let's go, David," Jason said.
"What do you chase her for?"

Jason stood up and got between David and Jon.
"Please, don't leave," Jon said. "David Grey is going to get the next round."

Jason took off with Grey. Grey's eyes were squinted and he was pale. Jon went on talking about David. I sat around and listened. Kelley looked upset.
"Jon, you might just give him a break," Kelley interrupted.
"I'm not on his side, of course, you're right." She looked at me.

Jon wasn't as animated anymore and it was just us as friends sitting at the table now.
"I'm not as hammered as you might think."
"I know," Kelley said.
"None of us are sober," I said.
"Well I meant everything I said."
"There's a time and a place for everything, though, Jon."
"But what a jackass he is. He followed us out to La Quinta when he knew full well he wasn't welcome there. He followed Kelley around and just stared at her. It made me absolutely sick. It was disgusting."
"He wasn't in very good form," Kelley said.

"Mind you, Kelley has had her men before. She's told me about them. She forwarded me this guy's email, too. I deleted them all."
"How honest of you."
"No, check this out Jack. Kelley has had her men. But they were never cops and they didn't ever follow her around afterwards."
"Oh, great, guys," Kelley said. "It's crap to talk about this. Jon and I have a good arrangement."
"She forwarded all of his emails to me. I deleted them."
"You didn't read my email either, baby. You deleted them too."
"I hate email," Jon said, "Sort of ironic, isn't it?"
"You don't read anything, do you?"
"Well you're wrong there. I read plenty of things online and plenty of books when I'm at work."
"Before you know it you'll be writing emails," Kelley said. "Well Jonathan, suck it up. You've made your bed and now you have to sleep in it. David is here, and we're all here, and you can't ruin the party for everyone."
"Tell him to be cool, then."
"He'll be alright. I'll talk to him."
"Jack, you can tell him to be cool. Tell him to chill or get out of here."
"Yeah," I said. "It would be perfect for me to talk with him about you."
"Kelley. Tell Jack what Grey says to you. That is really *great*, by the way."
"I can't even go there. It's incredible."
"I'll tell him, then."
"Don't be an ass, Jon."
"He tells her that he loves her and that he's going to marry her and father her children."

"He'd be a good father, you know," Kelley said. "He really believes in the whole marriage thing."
"I damned well do, too, you know."
"Hey, we'd better get something to eat," I said.
"What should I do when we see Grey?"
"Just pretend nothing happened."
"Fine with me," Jon said. "I meant what I said."
"Just tell him you were drunk if he brings it up."
"Cool. And you know, I just may have been a bit drunk."
"Let's go," Kelley said. "Are these drinks paid for? I've got to take a shower before dinner."

We walked across the pool area. The lights were on and it was quiet and dark. They went up to their rooms and I stopped to talk with Tina, who I spotted in the lobby.
"Well, what did you think of the bands?" she asked.
"O.K. they were solid musicians."
"They were O.K." – Tina shook her head – "but they're not that good."
"What didn't you like?"
"I'm not sure. They just didn't get me to the place I thought they would."
"I think I know what you mean."
"They were OK."
"Agreed. They were OK."
"How did your friends like them?"
"They thought they were great."
"Mmmm hmm."

I went back to my room. Jason was in his suite out on the balcony smoking a cigarette and looking at the pool. I went over next to him.
"Where did Grey go?"
"Up to his room."
"Is he O.K?"

"Just as you would expect. Jon was really pretty bad. He's a bad drunk."

"He wasn't that drunk."

"Yeah right. I was matching him before we met up with you guys."

"Well he sobered up quick."

"Good. That was a scene and a half. Obviously, I'm not hot no Grey, and it was disgusting for him to go along to La Quinta, but nobody should talk like Jon."

"How did you like the bands?"

"Awesome. It's great the way they're playing here."

"Tomorrow we have a couple more."

"When does the big tour start?"

"Couple of days."

"We've got to cut Jon off before he gets out of control again. I can't stand scenes like that."

"Hey, we'd better get ready for dinner."

"Yes, indeed. I'm sure it will be a wonderful dinner."

"Yeah."

And indeed, dinner was excellent. Kelley wore a short black skirt and a white halter-top. She looked very elegant. Jon pretended nothing had happened earlier. I went up to David's room to bring him down. He was polite and a bit formal, and he was diminished, but finally his spirits rose. He couldn't take his eyes off of Kelley. Looking at Kelley made his spirits rise and it must have been nice to see her looking so perfect, and know that he had been with her and that everyone else now knew it. This was something he would always have. Jason was hilarious and made everyone laugh. And so was Jon. They had the whole table laughing.

It was like certain parties we had before we came out to The 909. There was lots of wine and booze, and we chose to ignore any tension there was between us over Kelley. Beneath the wine and cocktails I found that I was feeling all right and forgot about how depressed and disgusted the whole world had made me. For a minute it was like we were all just a group of good friends.

CHAPTER FOURTEEN

I'm not sure what time I got to bed that night. I remember throwing my clothes on the chair, putting on some sweats, and having a smoke out on the balcony. I remember being pretty drunk, and when I sat down on the bed to go to sleep the world started to spin on me. I had a monster headache. I remember sitting there trying to read a short story by Richard Feynman, thinking to myself that the story was somehow familiar, but I had never read it so it was brand new to me at the time. The world seemed to come into focus very clearly and the pain in my head started to subside. I really was very drunk and I knew that if I stopped reading and closed my eyes I would get the spins and get sick. I hated to get sick. I knew that if I kept on reading that feeling would go away.

I heard some noise in the hall and it was Kelley and David Grey coming back to their rooms. Grey said good night to Kelley outside my door and he went upstairs to his room. I heard Kelley go into the next room. Jon was already asleep. We had come in together an hour or so ago.

I'm sure he woke up as she came in and I heard them talking. Then they were laughing. I turned my lights off and tried to go to sleep. My head was feeling a little better and I didn't have to read any more. I shut my eyes and the world straightened out. But I couldn't fall asleep. I was drunk, and when I drink I always get depressed. I always get depressed at night, too. Things always look different in the dark. There's no reason that things should be worse at night than they are in the daytime, but when it comes to just about anything, it's always worse at night. I tried to tell myself that it was just the booze, and that it would all be better in the morning. Yeah right.

Once upon a time I figured out that I didn't get so blue if there was a little light on. So I never turned the lights off when I went to sleep. This lasted for about a year. What a great idea. Women should all go to hell, anyway. So should you, Kelley Taylor. Go to hell.

But women always made such great friends didn't they? Really great, yeah. First of all, you had to be physically attracted to a woman in some way to want to be her friend at all in the first place. If you weren't attracted to her, why would you even talk to her, much less want her as a friend? And I had *always* considered Kelley a friend. I never thought about what *she* might be thinking about things between us. I'm pretty sure all women are different from men in this regard. With regard to relationships, that is. I was getting her friendship without paying for it in the usual way. There was no exchange. Not like the usual exchange where the woman gives something and you give something else back. There was no give and take; there was no quid pro quo. My father told me once that if something's too good to be true, than it is. Well, here it was. This was too good to be true. I guess with men and women who end up together forever, the each of them get something that they want from the other person. And I think it's very rarely the same thing. I guess I had tricked myself into thinking that it had to be the same thing, and would brush off girls who didn't see in me what I saw in them. It was sort of like what happens when you get some money and start to buy things. And then what you do with those things that you get. Well, I've come up with some theories in my time, and these seemed pretty good. I don't think people are smarter when they drink or take drugs; it's just that their amazement threshold goes down. All of the inane bullshit just seems so damn profound. Tomorrow this will seem as inane as all of the other theories I've come up with.

Well maybe it wasn't true, though. Maybe as you go along in life you do learn some things about girls and about money and about life. And you go along and you live as a better person after you learn these things and you learn from your mistakes and you can be happy about them. I didn't care about all of that. I just wanted to live. I didn't want to die young. I didn't want to die at all.

I wished Jon wouldn't be so bad about David Grey. Jon was a bad drunk. Kelley was an excellent drunk. Jason was a good drunk. David never got drunk. Jon was just really bad after a certain point. I did enjoy seeing him hurt Grey, though. I wished he wouldn't do it, though, because when it was done I felt disgusted about life. I guess that was what having morals was supposed to be like, things that made you feel disgusted and guilty about life afterwards. No, that must be something that is immoral. Oh, the things that I could come up with at night. It was all a load of crap. Oh Bollocks, I could hear Wright say. Oh, Bollocks! When you hang around people from other countries you get into the habit of thinking with their expressions. The English language has so few words that people actually use. It probably has less useable words than Hawaiian does. Of course, I don't know Hawaiian, and I don't think anyone alive does either. We did a good job of wiping that right out, we American's did. But anyhow, people use so few words these days. It's all good. Right on. No worries. People use empty language.

I turned the lights on in the hotel room and started to read again. I read Feynman. I knew that reading now, in my drunken state of mind that somehow I would remember his words and it would seem as if his stories had happened to me. That was highly moral. I think I fell asleep some time after the sun came up.

The next two days in Palm Desert were pretty quiet, and there weren't any more fights. They were getting ready for the concert down at the polo fields, and the hotel started to swell with visitors for the event. Out at Coachella, the workers built concessions, parking areas, and the stages started to become recognizable.

Each morning I could go down for breakfast at about 11:00am, and read the Times and then I would walk around the hotel enjoying the cool air and atmosphere. Jason came along. Other times he stayed in his room working, reading. Kelley and Jon were never seen before noon. We all drank margaritas at the poolside bar. We were all content and no one was too drunk. I made my way into Palm Springs a couple of times, once with Kelley. Once we stopped in at the Catholic Church. She wanted to say all of the prayers, but it was too much to teach her in the quiet atmosphere of the church and she wouldn't understand the significance of them anyhow. When we came back to the hotel, Grey was obviously waiting for us at the bar adjacent to the main

entrance of the hotel. He wanted to go to lunch at a very good place, and we agreed to join him. Then we were side tracked, and ended up at a bar that looks like a red barn, and we all went next door and had our palms read in a seedy room before lunch. All of us were well, and we felt good, and I felt all right about Grey. It was hard to feel anything but good on a day like that.
It was the last day before Coachella.

CHAPTER FIFTEEN

On May 9^h – Thursday -- the crowds exploded into the polo grounds and they didn't stop coming for four days. People had been driving in from L.A. all week, but they were spread out at all the hotels in Palm Desert and Palm Springs, and you didn't notice the crowd so much. The fields were as hot as they were on any other day. You could see the local casino and run down motel workers getting ready for the concert. It was probably good seasonal work for them. The people from out of town were getting started slowly, drinking beer they had brought in, store bought, rather than paying concession prices, and they looked very shy about things. They needed some time to make the shift in moral values slowly, and they wanted to get drunk cheaply on store bought beer rather than get killed at the concessions. At this point they still knew the value of the dollar – as the concert went on, value would blur and price wouldn't matter. They would charge $10.00 for a bottle of water and people would gladly pay for it. Other values would blur as well.

Now, on the first day of the Coachella Music festival at the polo field in Indio, the people had been in their cars all day driving in from Orange County and Los Angeles, some coming in from hotels in Palm Springs, Palm Desert, Indian Wells, and they were drinking their store bought beer. I could hear their radios playing in their cars, and they were having tailgate parties, drinking the beer and smoking the pot they had brought from home. They were parked on the side of the road and in dusty lots leading up to the venue. They were playing their favorite music on their car stereos and they all were wearing different shirts and shoes and pants, and especially wild hair, and you could tell what sort of scene they were into. People indeed were just getting started. Coachella is a music festival.

It was just a little after noon when I parked my car in a good spot and got out to join David Grey and Jason at a tailgate party they had been invited to by these guys that started a website called (909) pride. Nice guys. I parked and got out of my car, and walked over past several large groups of people. There were metal stakes and yellow nylon rope, which marked the proper places to drive and to park. The polo fields had been prepared for the frenzy. The local workers weren't as relaxed as they had been the previous week, taking time to stop and chat. Now they were directing traffic and yelling at people who wouldn't follow their directions. I arrived at a large group of people hanging around a large truck.

"What are you guys drinking?" I asked David and Jason.
"Tequila," Grey said.
"Patron?" I asked Jason. He cocked his head at me, "Now, now, Jack."

Before the guy serving the drinks could tell me he had my shot ready, the first band started in on a heavy distorted guitar chord that was louder than anyone expected. The chord exploded and the look on everyone's face changed and looked around as the chord hung in the air and slowly faded down to the ground. By the time the intro of the song was over, the guy handing me my tequila had to dance around and through the crowd of people that were now rushing into the concert area from their tailgate parties. People were coming into the entrance from all directions and we could hear people's excitement, the girls holding each other hands, and guys drinking beer out of cans, and all of them shouting and screaming. When the band went into the verse everyone was walking and talking and laughing and the bass was loud and the drums were sharp and high, and as the players went into the chorus again, everyone would holler and the girls would yell, "wooooooo!" It was crowded and you could now only see the heads and shoulders of people going up and down.

There was an older man with extremely bad skin, wearing a loose black tank top and a backward foam and nylon baseball cap that read, "Show me your BOOB," on it. He had an old style ghetto blaster on his shoulder playing some music and he was dancing around, and small crowds of people were following him into the concert cheering at him and his antics.

"Look at that guy, he must be touched in the head," Jason said.

"HEY SKETCHER" someone called out.

There was a largish crowd of people, all guys over towards the parking lot that had their own PA set up and they were talking on the microphone. They also had a large banner stemming between the hitches of their two trucks that read, "The 909 rocks! 909 Pride! Go dirt people!" They were drinking and having a great time and everyone was happy.

"What are dirt people?" David asked.

"We're the dirt people," Jason replied.

The whole time you could hear a band playing, perhaps warming up for one of the sets that would happen later on. The parking lot was full, and people were at their tailgates and they were pouring into the festival area.

"Where's Kelley and Jon," Jason asked.

"I know where they are," Grey said.

"So go get them."

The festival was now officially happening. It would keep going, day and night, for four days. The people were dancing, drinking, smoking, playing music, and partying, and they wouldn't stop for four days. Everything that happened here could only happen at this festival. The event became unreal and finally it seemed like no action could have any real consequence. It didn't seem right to think about consequence or morals or right or wrong at any time during the festival. All the time, even when things were sort of quiet, it felt like you had to yell to get something heard. And it was the same about any action. If you did something, you had to go big. It was a big party, and it went on for four days.

That afternoon, the radio DJs from the big local radio station set up their booth and started broadcasting live from the event. Super Steve Florez was there. Super Steve is a local radio personality in Los Angeles, and we happened to go to school together. He wondered why I was hanging out here with the Dirt People. He knew about my background and often asked me what I was doing living out in Riverside. All of the artists playing gave interviews with the DJs. The crowd was too large around the radio grandstand area, watching the bands, some of them were national or even international celebrities, and it was especially hectic when they started to broadcast live. You couldn't see them because there were too many people around. There was a group of people wearing red shirts, and they were all with the radio station. They had set up a large booth with inflatable palm trees which were thirty feet tall, and some other large inflatable structures, including a swimming pool and a castle, like you see at kid parties.

There were people standing all around the radio booth, crowding the small stage. We were at a tailgate party that someone with the radio station had set up nearby to look like a bar. Kelley had taken a seat on the arm of some occupied chair. It was bright and hot outside by the makeshift bar, and the drunks all around were singing along to a Sublime song that was playing on their radio. There were girls dancing and pulling on all of the guys that were willing to dance with them. They kept pulling Corona's out of a cooler they had behind their bar. Using them to chase tequila they had in a bota-bag.

"I want one of those," Jason said.

"I know those guys back at 909 pride," I said. "I'll go get us some booze."

The girls didn't want to let me get away. Three of them went around the chair that Kelley was sitting on and put several of those plastic flower leis around her neck. Someone gave her a shot and a Corona. Then someone was showing Jason how to open a beer with a plastic cigarette lighter. Shouting the instructions into his ear and clapping him on the back encouragingly.

I told everyone that I'd be back. Out on the main path towards the venue I went up to where some vendors were selling all sorts of different things and saw someone on the other side of the trail with some of those old-70's style bota-bags. The crowd was pushing it's way up the main artery into the show area and I pushed my way through and up beyond where they would check your tickets. It smelled good, like someone was barbequing and I stopped in at this little booth with the bota-bags. I pointed at several of them that were hanging on pegs up and down the supports of the booth and the guy took them down and showed me that they were new.
"Check it out."
"Can you grab me that big one up there? I want to pick up a couple of these things."
"Going to put some wine in 'em?"
"Booze."
He smiled and shook my hand.
"Good man. Forty bucks for the both of them. Won't find a better deal."
The guy at the cash register checking out folks whistled and nodded his head.
"Good deal my man, forty bucks."
    I paid the guy and elbowed my way back into the crowd, back down past the radio booth to our tailgate party. The party had swelled and it was hotter than ever, and they had pitched a tent. I didn't see Kelley or Jason, and someone said they were over at the radio booth. We went over to the truck and brought out the tequila. One bag held a full bottle of straight booze, and the other we filled with a makeshift margarita mixture of tequila, sweet and sour mix, and limejuice. The guy with the Tequila wouldn't let me pay for the bottles at first, but I finally gave him a couple of

twenties, and he brought out another bottle and we took two shots a piece from his tequila. I offered him the margarita mixture and he mouthed the bottle and chased his shots.

"Yeah, boy," he shouted and handed the bag back to me. Some of it got on his shirt, but he didn't notice at all.

Back over by the radio booth and bar Kelley and Jason were sitting together on the chair, in the middle of a dance circle. Everyone was switching partners every so often and grinding and hugging and stealing kisses. Jon was sitting Indian style with a bunch of guys with their shirts off, sitting around a little hibachi with carne asada roasting over the coals. It smelled really good.

"Hey, Jack! Hey!" Jon called. "Sit down over here – come on man. Meet our new friends. We're having some tacos."

Jon introduced me to all of the guys around the grill "Stop stealing their beef, Jonathan," Kelley yelled over from her chair by the bar.

"No, no, that's OK. I don't want to eat your dinner," I said when someone handed me the tongs to fix myself a taco.

"Come on man, that's what we made it for! Come on! Go ahead."

I took the cap off the tequila, passed it first, and then the margarita mix, which went over really well with everyone, and everyone had a shot or two.

Over by the main stage we could hear another band starting up.

"Isn't that the band?" Jon asked.

"No way," someone said, "They're just getting ready, drink up!"

"They finally found you."

"Someone helped me find you guys," Jon said. "They told me that you'd be here."

"Where's Grey?"
"Assed out," Kelley yelled, "They put him down somewhere."
"Where exactly?"
"How should I know?" Jason said. "I think someone capped his ass."
"Nobody shot him," Jon said. "I know he's not shot. He's just passed out on the Jager."

As he said Jager a guy over at the truck looked over, grabbed a bottle out of the cooler and tossed it over to me.
"Oh man," I said, "No thanks!"
"Oh yes. Yes! Yes, you have to! Drink! Bottoms up now."

I took a deep, cool, swig. It tasted like licorice and I could feel it going down cool and then a sweet aftertaste. I felt it warming up my stomach.
"Where in hell is Grey?"
"I have no idea," Jon said. "I'll ask around. Where is that passed out bastard?" he asked everyone.
"You want to check on him?"
"Yeah," I said.
"Not this kid," Jon said, "This guy over here."

The guy with the Jager wiped his mouth on the neck part inside of his shirt, pulling it straight up to his face and over his mouth, sighed, and stood up.
"Over here."

In the camping tent that they had set up to store various party gear, David Grey was sleeping quietly on a sleeping bag. It was almost too hot to enter the tent. They had some clothes bundled up to put under his head. Around his neck were bunches of those plastic flower leis, all different colors.
"Let him sleep it off," the guy whispered to me. "He's cool here."

THE 909

A couple of hours later Grey emerged from the tent sweating. He came out to the front of the truck, still with the plastic leis around his neck. The guys all yelled for him when he came out. Grey blinked his eyes, rubbed them, and smiled.

"Must have dozed off there for a while," he said.

"Oh yeah, right," Kelley said.

"You had a cap in yo ass," Jason said.

"Aren't we going back to get something to eat?" Grey said.

"You want to eat?"

"Yeah, sure. I can always eat."

"Eat those flowers, David," Jon said. "Hey, eat those flower leis."

David just stood there. His sleep had put him pretty straight.

"Yes, let's go get some food," Kelley said. "I've got to take a shower."

We said our goodbyes to all of the folks at the tailgate party and at the radio booth, and the bar, and we shook everyone's hands and got many sweaty hugs. It was getting dark.

"What time do you suppose it is?" Grey asked.

"It's Sunday, " Jon said. "You've been asleep for two days."

"Seriously," said Grey, "What time is it?"

"About ten."

"Man we drank a lot."

"You mean *we* drank a lot. You passed out."

Driving out of the dusty parking lot we watched some fireworks go off back at the concert area. Through the long rows of parked cars, we could see people at their tailgate parties, illuminated in the dark by the amber light from within their cars.

We all ate too much back at the hotel. And the prices were always double eating at a hotel. We were up all night drinking and dancing at the club and I remember resolving to myself that I would make it to the show before 10:00am so that I wouldn't miss any of the bands, and I was worn out from the day so I went to sleep at about four o'clock. Everyone else stayed out.

I couldn't find the card key to my room – I had several, but none of them worked, so I went over to the room that Grey had and one of the cards worked on his door and I slept in one of the beds in Grey's room. The party was going on outside all night, but I was too worn out for it to keep me awake. When I woke up it was the heat of the day and the sound of the air conditioner, and the people walking past the room – which announced the start of the day – people were leaving to go to festival. I had been fast asleep and woke up with that terrible feeling of being late. I pulled on my boxers and went out onto the balcony. The good spots were already taken down at the pool. I was sure that I was going to be too late to round everyone up and make it to the polo grounds in time to see all of the bands. So I went back to bed.

Grey woke me up when he came into the room. He started to get undressed and went over and closed to curtains because the people at the pool were looking in.
"Anything interesting happen?" I asked.
"Yes, we were all out all night."
"Anyone fight?"
"Some guy came up to Jason and Jon kicked him."
"Did Kelley have a good time?"
"We were all drunk and dancing and partying all night. The little scuff was so short it didn't bother anyone."
"I wish I could have been there."

"Everyone was asking where you were. We checked your room, too, but it was locked and nobody answered."
"Where do you guys stay out?"
"We were dancing at the club downstairs."
"I was beat," I said.
"Man, I'm beat now," Grey said. "Does the party ever stop?"
"Not for four days."
Jason opened the door and stuck his head in.
"Where the hell were you Jack?"
"Have a good time?"
"Excellent."
"Where you headed?"
"Bed."

Nobody was awake before two o'clock. We ate at the café down by the water. The hotel was full of people. We had to sign in for a table. We finally got on our way to the festival and headed over to our tailgate party. The tailgate parties got more crowded as the time came for the real show to begin. There was a buzz to the talk that went on and there was a different noise somehow that the crowd made as the time got closer. The buzz went on, and we were a part of the buzz.

I had six really good tickets for the festival. Three of them were pit tickets, the area right in front of the stage, and three were orchestra, towards the front of the amphitheater. Jon thought Kelley had better sit high up, and Grey wanted to sit with them. Jason and I were going to be in the pit, and so I scalped the extra pit ticket. Jason was telling Grey something about one of the bands and how to get into the pit. Telling him how to sneak past the security guards. He had been here once before.

"I'm not worried about getting kicked out. I'm only afraid I'll be bored and want to leave."
"Oh, yeah?"
"If you fall down in the pit, cover your head and face," I told Kelley. "Try to get back on your feet before you do anything else. People here are pretty nice. They'll help you out."
"She'll be alright. I'll watch her."
"I'm going to rush the pit, and I'll be down with you guys in no time," Kelley said.
"I don't think you're going to be bored," Jason said.
"I'm going to the lounge," I said. "See you in the pit. Don't get trashed."
"I'm coming," Jason said. Kelley smiled at us.

We walked up the amphitheater and around the booths to avoid the beating sun.
"Grey really kills me," Jason said. "He's got that blue collar cop superiority complex now so much that he thinks that the only way he's going to feel about this show is bored."
"We'll keep an eye on him," I said.
"Oh F him," Jason said.
"He does that to himself all the time."
"Well he can keep on."
At the VIP lounge and bar we met up with Steve Florez.
"Hey guys, you want to meet Travis Barker?"
"Great," said Jason. "Let's go."

We followed Steve around and thru several rooms and doors. He's in the green room getting ready for a show he's doing with a side project.

Steve knocked on the door and opened it up. It was a shabby portable structure we were in, but it was set up as a bedroom and hospitality suite. There were two beds in

the room as well as a catered lunch and beer and sodas. The guy stood up and not smiling in his wife beater and cutoffs. A chain ran down out of one pocket and was connected to his shorts with a clip. He was drinking water out of a small plastic bottle. He had shaved his head bald and it was shiny under the fluorescent lights. Travis Barker nodded at us both and he seemed very far away, and in his own world. Steve said something about we were writers and in the press and how big of fans we were and that we wanted to wish him well before the show. Then he looked over at me. He cut the most intimidating figure that I have ever seen.
"You're going to check out the show today?" he said.
"Yes, you know not everyone can appreciate this project, " I said, feeling stupid."
"No," he said.

There were some publicity people over at the catering table, with their mouths full, and they came over to us interrupting to make sure their guy didn't say anything he wasn't supposed to for the press. "Is there anything that you'd like to ask Mr. Barker?" He was twenty-seven years old and had dropped out of high school in his junior year to play in Blink 182 and he wasn't playing for Blink today, but another side project. We wished him to "break a leg," shook hands, and he was standing alone in the room with all of his groupies as we shut the door.
"He's a good kid, isn't he?" Steve asked.
"Impressive looking kid," I said.
"He looks like a rock star," Steve said. "He's that type of guy."
"He's a good kid."
"We'll see how the crowd is."

We found the bar in the VIP lounge, ordered several shots and beers, drank the shots, and went back to the pit.

It was a good show. Jason and I were excited to see the drummer that we had just met. Steve was sitting back stage. After the first song was over Steve caught my eye and nodded his head. Several times during the show I turned around and tried to find Jon and Kelley and Grey. They looked all right. Kelley didn't look tired or daunted or bored. All three were sitting on the backs of their chairs.
"Is that them," Jason said.
"Does Grey look bored to you?"
"That pig!"

In front of the stage, after the band was done, you couldn't move in the crowd. We tried, but couldn't make our way back through but had to move along with the whole crowd slowly like an iceberg back to the concession area. We had that slight let down feeling that comes right after a great band plays, and the feeling of euphoria that comes right after a good band plays. The festival was going on. People were whooping and drinking and laughing everywhere we turned. There were some girls dancing to the filler music they were playing. Finally we found our way out of the thick of the crowd and went towards the lounge.
"How old do you suppose that girl over there is?"
"Sixteen."
"Don't even joke with me about that."
"They all look the same to me. After college I've had a really hard time guessing a girl's age."
"Yeah, but you'd hit that."
"Don't even joke me."
"They're really good dancers."

We could watch the dancers from within the lounge, so we did, and the three of these girls were dancing and we were watching. They liked to have an audience. Then they were kissing each other.

"I like this sort of dancing."

Then the song stopped and the moment was gone and the girls blushed and laughed and continued up the way to the concessions.

"There's the crew," Jason said.

They were crossing over to the lounge.

"Hey guys!" I said.

"Hello gentlemen!" said Kelley. "You saved us some seats, how sweet."

"Hey," Jon said, "that Barker wha'sshisname's pretty good. Am I right?"

"Yeah, he's a hottie," Kelley said. "And those tattoos. Damn."

"Kelley never took her eyes off of them."

"I've got to come up into the pit tomorrow with you guys. Or get some binoculars."

"How do you like it so far?"

"It's awesome. Perfect. Isn't this great you guys?"

"How about the crowd?"

"There's so much going on. I can't stop checking everyone out."

"She couldn't take her eyes off them," Jon said, "what a tart."

"There are some crazy looking kids here," Kelley said.

"Having a good time, then, Kelley? You weren't bored?" Jason said.

"David Grey was," Jon added. "You were out of your mind, weren't you?"

"Well there were some songs that I didn't know," Grey said.

"Were you bored?" Jason asked.

Grey rolled his eyes.

"No. I wasn't bored. I'll never live that down will I?"

"It's cool," Jason said, "so long as you weren't bored."

"He didn't look like he was bored," Jon said. "I thought he was going to pop from enthusiasm."

"I wasn't that bad. Just for the songs I didn't know.'

"I thought that I was going to pop with enthusiasm. You weren't bored were you, David?"

"Drop it, Jon. I told you I was sorry I said that."

"He was bored, you know. Bored stiff."

"You shouldn't ever get bored at your first music festival, David," Jon said. "It would be such a disaster."

"Oh give it a rest Jonathan."

"He said that Kelley was into S&M," Jon said. "She's not into S&M, she's just a beautiful, wonderful tart."

"Are you into S&M Kelley?"

"I don't think so."

"He just said Kelley was into S&M because she likes the ties that bind her."

It was good that Jon and Jason got started on something other than David Grey. The waitress brought over the glasses with tequila shots.

"So you really liked it?" Jason asked Grey.

"I can't say that I liked it per se. It's a good show."

"Hell yes it's a good show!" Kelley said.

"I wish they played more songs that I know," Grey said.

"That's not important," Jason said. "After a while you can get into all of the songs."

"It's tough at the beginning," Kelley said.

"The band was good," Grey said.

"They were really good," Jon said.

"I want to be in the pit when we go back," Kelley took her shot.

"She wants to see the rock stars up close," Jon said.
"Oh yeah, they're something. That Barker is just a kid, though."
"He's a damned impressive kid," I said. "We were up in the green room, and we met him, and I've never seen such an impressive looking kid."
"How old do you think he is?"
"Twenty-six or twenty-seven."
"Just think about it."

The rest of the bands that played that day were good, and many were some of my favorite bands from the 80's. Now they are looked on as retro, slightly ridiculous, and slightly relevant. But it was good to hear to tunes and see the fading stars. I took Kelley and Jon down into the pit with me, and Jason and Grey were up in the orchestra seats. When Travis Barker came back onto the stage, Kelley couldn't stop talking about him and pointing him out to me. She told me that he was opening a Wahoo's in Norco. They sell fish tacos. I was telling her about the other bands and how some of them have evolved and about their music and the times and trends and fashion and she only wanted to talk about Travis Barker. He stayed out of the limelight, never pandering to his audience or acting badly. He was a real rock star. She knew why she liked him and none of the other performers. He had a sublime sense of self-confidence and superiority that the other performers did not have. I told her that lots of these musicians had to sell out and produce work that they didn't believe in.
"I'd never see him doing something like that. He'd get out before it came to that," Kelley said.
"He won't until his records stop selling," I said.
"They never will," Kelley said, "they're too damned good."

"He had talent right from the beginning, it's true. You can't learn talent. You've got to have the tickets."

"And he's damned good looking," Kelley said.

"I believe, my friends, that she is falling in love with this rock star guy," Jon said.

"It wouldn't surprise me."

"Do me a favor, Jack, be a good man and don't tell her anything else about this guy, his band or his music. Tell her that he's a heroin addict, a dead beat dad, and rapist or something."

"He sure does look like it," Kelley said.

"He does, doesn't he?"

"No he doesn't," Kelley said. She moved forward to get closer to the stage and away from Jon. After the show was over we were all pressed tightly to one another again. "These rock stars will tire a girl out," Kelley said, "I'm as dry as a leaf."

"You'll get a drink in you, " Jon said.

That night Travis Barker wouldn't play. A girl band was headlining, and a pretty obscure one at that. There weren't any bands that I had planned on watching. But the partying kept on going all day and all night.

CHAPTER SIXTEEN

The next morning it was cloudy. Clouds had crept in somehow and created a humidity that compared to dry heat was not very pleasant. It gets very hot here, but the dry heat is good heat that is easier to stand. You couldn't see the top of San Jacinto. The valley was dark, and the cactus and Joshua trees were different in the shade. I walked away from the hotel, out on the golf course to take a look at the weather. The clouds were coming in from the West. For a desert it sure does rain here.

The banners and lights outside and all around the hotel were damp against the side of the hotel, and during the steady hum from bugs and life that had come alive in the humidity you could hear the silence of a really hot heat. At Coachella, the party kept up without interruption, only in the heat it was driven mad with thirst and it was forced to take its clothes off.

The seats in the amphitheater had been crowded with people watching the show, and with people sneaking into better seats.
    Every now and again you'd see an argument over who had the rights to a seat, and ushers were not needed often to adjudicate. People were generally good-natured about these sorts of things. We got caught, and we'll move. Sorry about that. The score evens out. The crowd was waiting in line for beer, eating plates of Chinese food, waiting in line for water, and standing around laughing and talking. It was hot and now it was humid. I left the crowd and went back to the hotel to get cleaned up and to get ready for a dinner we had planned. I started to shave in my room when someone knocked at the door.
"Come on in," I yelled.
Super Steve Florez walked in.
"How are you doing?" he said.
"Fine," I said.
"No important shows today."
"No," I said, "nothing but humidity."
"Where are all of your friends?"
"Downstairs in the restaurant."
Florez smiled his understanding and sarcastic smile.
"Listen," he said. "Do you know Commie Girl?"
"Um, yeah," I said. "Everyone knows Commie Girl."
"She's here in town."
"Yeah," I said. "Everyone's seen her."
"I've seen her, too," Florez said. He didn't say anything else. I continued shaving.
"Hey, why don't you have a seat, " I said, "Want to have a drink?"
"No, I've got to get back to the station."

THE 909

    I finished up shaving and dunked my whole head in the cold water. Steve was standing outside the bathroom, perhaps a bit uncomfortable.

"OK," he said. "I just got an email from Commie Girl that they want me, Travis, and you to come over to her suite for drinks after dinner tonight."

"Well, it can't hurt Travis any."

"They've been out at the casino all day, and I'm not sure that he'll make it back by tonight. And if they are … "

    Steve was fishing, and he wanted me to say something.

"Just don't pass the message on."

"You think?"

"Absolutely not. I'm positive."

Steve was relieved.

"I wanted to ask you because you have some experience with these things."

"That's my job."

"Yeah, you know – people take a kid like Barker, they don't know that he should stick to making music and not get involved too much with the media. Any press person can flatter the guy. They start this drinks after dinner business, and in a year they're through."

"Like L…"

"They're great people," I said. "There's one of my friends down there that collects rock stars."

"I know, and they only want the famous ones."

"Yah, the washed up ones get fat and don't have any money."

"Or they're on drugs."

"OK," I said, "it's simple. Just don't forward the email along, and don't pass the message to him personally."

"He's such a good kid, he ought to stick to his people. He doesn't need to get involved with that crowd."
"Why don't you have a beer with me?"
"No," said Florez, "I've got to get back to work." He left the room.

I went down the elevator to the lobby and took a walk thru the shops and down by the pool. It was still humid. I looked in at the café for my gang and nobody was there, so I walked over and around the pool again. They were eating dinner at the Japanese restaurant.

They were way ahead on drinks, and there was no way I could catch up with them. Jason was buying sake bombs for Jon. The waitress kept bringing them over.
"This is the eleventh bomb I'm going to take, why the hell not make it a dozen!" Jon said. "Jason you're an ass."
Evidently Jason was tipping very liberally and the news had spread to the other cocktail waitresses.
"Another drink?" she said to Jason.
"No,' Jason said, "not for me. For him."
The waitress left quickly to go get another round.

I was drinking a large bottle of Sapporo, and I was so far behind that I was slightly embarrassed by their antics. I looked around the room. Two tables over was Travis Barker. When I nodded, he stood up and waved me over to meet a friend of his. His table was two down and so I got up and walked over there. His friend was a New York art critic, a very beautiful, trim brunette. I told Travis how much I enjoyed his set and he was happy to hear it. We talked about rock and the critic knew a little bit about music herself, and I excused myself to go back and get my beer from the table and she grabbed my waist with both hands from behind and pulled me back down into my seat. Barker laughed.

"Drink with us," she said.

She was a little bit shy talking about herself, but she was very pleased with her knowledge and experience with art and music and travel, and she was cautious talking about places that she thought we never had been to or bands that maybe we hadn't heard of. She was anxious to hear about the local music scene, and what it was like living in the Inland Empire and growing up in Orange County. We equated everything to her New York version of New Jersey. Everyone claimed New Jersey was backwards and the people were different. Much the same happens in Southern California between Los Angeles, Orange County, and the Inland Empire. It was sort of a stratification based on your geography and your area code. Based on where you live or where you grew up.

Travis Barker mentioned that he grew up in Rancho Cucamonga, and that was not far from Riverside compared with Los Angeles. And as far as he was concerned, he would stay there and he had purchased a house in the area. The critic joked him that it sure wasn't L.A., and it damned sure wasn't New York. He said that he had been to New York with his parents when he was nineteen years old and he had hated it. But he didn't hate this hotel or other fancy, fast-paced places. We started to talk about his band and I mentioned that I had seen them three times before. It was only twice, but by the time the conversation had come back around, I didn't want to have to explain myself. But I had seen them enough and read about their shows so I was O.K. "Where were you the last time? The Weenie Roast?"

"Yes," that wasn't true, but I read about a riot they had incited at the show.

"The first or the second time?"

"The first time."

"Ah, so you were in the riot."
"That was great."
He went over the story of how they had told everyone to disregard the security guards, and hundreds of people ran right up to the front of the stage. He also joked about how they had told everyone to throw some trash. I offered that I had been hit with some half eaten buffalo wings, and my friend got hit in the ear by a quarter.
"I'm anxious to see you guys tomorrow," the critic said.
"Just wait. It'll be good."
"Hey Jack, are you too good for us now?" Kelley called from the other table.
"It's just temporary."
"You *are* better than us."
"Tell him that their new album sucks," Jon shouted. He was totally drunk.
Travis looked at me with raised eyebrows.
"Wasted," I said. "He's hammered."
"You *could* introduce your friends," Kelley said. She hadn't stopped looking at Barker. I asked them if they wanted to have a drink with us. Both the critic and Barker stood up to meet my friends. They had very good manners and were very good with people. There were introductions all around and there weren't enough seats for everyone to sit down so we moved to the big table by the window to have more drinks. Jason ordered a bottle of cold sake and glasses for everyone. There was a lot of happy excited drunk talking.
"You can tell everyone you know that I'm embarrassed to be a writer," Jason said. "Go ahead, you can spread the word."
Travis was laughing and the New York critic was having fun. It wasn't work any more.

"This gentleman to my left is also a writer. A brilliant and quite accomplished writer."

Barker was impressed. "The other one isn't," thumbing over to Grey.

"He looks like Anthony Keatis," Barker said, looking at Jason. "OH SHIT," he said, "Now I know why you look familiar. You were a manager there when I used to work at Target in Rancho."

"Garden Section?" Jason asked.

"YES," Barker answered "Oh No! What a small world."

I was sure they wouldn't recognize each other. But they did.

"Tell him that Kelley wants to see his tattoos."

"Jon, man. Shut it."

"Tell him that she's dying to see how she can get to see his tattoos."

"Shut it."

During all of this Barker was drinking beer out of a long bottle and talking with Kelley. Kelley was smiling and talking quietly and he was looking cool and confident and they were laughing.

Jason had more beers brought around.

"Tell him that Kelley wants to -----"

"For the love of god and man!"

Barker looked up with a smile on his face, "God and man. Are you quoting David Bowie now?" He was talking and laughing with Kelley. Just then Steve Florez walked into the room he started to smile at me, then he saw Travis Barker with a big bottle of beer in his hand, sitting laughing by me and two very nice looking girls at a table filled with loud drunk people. He didn't even give a nod.

Florez went out of the dining room. Jon was hoisting a glass and standing with one foot on a chair proposing a toast. "I'd like to propose a toast. Here's to ---" he started. "Travis Barker," I interrupted. We all touched glasses roughly and finished off the rest of our drinks. Travis looked happy to have been toasted, and I drank mine quickly having had to save the toast. Jon had made it clear that Travis wasn't at all what he was going to be drinking to. But it went off well, and it was time for everyone to split up, so, we all shook hands and Travis went off with his rock critic friend.

"Jesus he's great," Kelley said.

"I wonder if he's any good," Kelley said. "I wonder if he's with that girl from New York. He's probably a slut."

"I was going to tell him," Jon started to say, "but Jack interrupted me. He's always interrupting people. Hey do you think you're better than people interrupting them all the time?"

"Christ, Jon, Nobody did anything to you."

"No, I like to settle this once and for all." He turned his back to me. "You do think quite highly of yourself, don't you Grey? Do you think you belong here with us? With us party people? Don't have too much fun, now, Grey, don't have too much for or anything."

"Come on, Jon," Grey said.

"Do you think Kelley wants you here? Do you think you add to the conversation or, the scenery or something, Grey?"

"I said all I had to say the other night, Jon."

"I'm not one of you guys." Jon stepped sideways and put his hand on the table, using it to hold himself up. "I may not care, but I know when I'm not wanted. You're a smart guy, Grey, can't you see when you're not wanted at a place? Get out of here. Go away. Nobody wants you here.

Take that sad blue-collar face back to Orange County. I'm right, aren't I?"
He raised his eyebrows at us all for approval.
"Yeah," I said, "Let's all go over to Bananaz."
"No. You know I'm right. I'm in love with that girl."
"Oh, don't even go there Jon," Kelley said.
"Seriously, I'm right, aren't I Jack?"
Grey was still sitting at the table. His face was sad and there were black rings around each of his eyes. You could see the color washing out of his face, but somehow when Jon threw these insults at him, somehow he was smiling and sort of waiting and enjoying it. It was like a middle school shoving contest over an insult, but with booze.
"Jack, seriously," he voice was shaking. "You of all people should know I'm right. Grey, you listen!" He slapped both of his hands on the table and sort of hunched over, bending down to look straight at Grey over the table, "Get out of here. Leave. Nobody wants you here!"
"But I'm not going anywhere, Jon," said Grey.
"Then I'll make your ass leave." Jon started to move around the table towards where Grey was sitting. Grey stood up right away and took his glasses off. He stood waiting; black circles around his eyes, standing with confidence but with his hands open and upturned as if asking why this was happening to him. But he was ready to fight for his love, Kelley, and it was clear to everyone that he was ready to do battle for her.
I grabbed Jon around his shoulders. "Come on, let's all get out of here," I said. "You can't do this here in the hotel."
"Yeah. Yeah, right."
We all headed out. Looking back I saw Jon stumbling over to the elevators and I saw Grey putting his

hands back down and putting his glasses back on. Jason was still sitting at the table with his bottle. Kelley was zoned out and looking straight ahead with her eyes open but not focused on anything.

Outside by the pool it had stopped raining and the moon was barely visible through the clouds. You could smell the fresh rain, and the grounds were steaming. There was some elevator music coming in on the loudspeaker and a bunch of kids were playing Marco Polo in the large swimming pool. Some were playing around trying to cover each other's eyes and they fell into the pool. You could tell they were all cheating. A girl would start out diving into the pool and pass very close to her friend. Then she would suddenly reach out to the right or to the left and tag her friend, obviously peeking under the water. They would explode with laughter and accuse each other of cheating and then whoever was tagged as it would climb out of the pool and start the game again.

Kelley came out with Jason and joined us. We sat over by the bar and watched the Marco Polo players, getting out of the pool, yelling, laughing, and then diving back into the water. There was no wind and the subsiding rain smelled nice and the weather was good. You could smell the chlorine and the salt from the new rain and the kids' faces were laughing and as they chased each other their feet slapped down on the wet pavement.

"They're playing Marco Polo," Jason said.

"How do you know they're playing Marco Polo," Kelley said.

"He's the name of the game, Marco Polo, fish out of water, No."

"Marco Polo," Jon said, "An Italian who knew a hell of a lot more about water than these kids."

The wind came up and blew the laughter away.
"Hey, I wish those kids would stop," Kelley said.
"They probably planned this game for weeks," Jason said.
"Marco Polo, Polo loco, un Poco loco amigo," Jon said.
"Let's go," Kelley said. "We can't sit here."
"The princess calls," Jon said.

The hotel club was crowded inside. Nobody noticed our arrival. There weren't any tables available. The music was too loud for conversation.
"Let's get out of here," Jason said.

Outside the arcade was busy with tourists and people in town for the festival – browsing at the uniquely desert fashion and junk shops, buy ice cream. The women were all dressed very nicely and were lousy with jewelry. Somehow we had acquired a new member in our group, one of Jason's friends. She was in Palm Desert for the weekend, staying with another girl at the hotel. Her friend had a headache and was sleeping.
"Here's the place," Jon said. It was the lobby bar, a small, well-appointed place with nice atmosphere where you could also order from the kitchen and small bands would play. We all found chairs around a table and sat down and ordered bottles of Heineken all around. The bar wasn't full. It was dead.
"This place is going off," Jason said.
"It's still early."
"Let's take our beer and go somewhere else. We shouldn't be here on a night like this."
"Let's go watch the French," Jon said. "I just love to watch them dance."
"Oh god, you're sick," Jason said, "Leave them alone. "I do wonder why they're here. Where do they all come from?"

"They come in from Palm Springs," Jon said. "They come to cruise and party with the beautiful people."
"They should go back to Palm Springs," Jason said. "Come on, let's go tell them to please go back to Palm Springs."
"You are absolutely gorgeous." Jon turned to Jason's friend. "How long have you been here?"
"Give it a rest Jon."
"Seriously, how beautiful is she? Tell me, isn't she the best-looking girl you've seen here? Is she cute or what? How sexy is this girl? Hey, come with Jason and me – we're going to tell the French to go back to France."
"I'll free those Frenchmen, Jason said, "What are they doing here in America?"
"Let's go," Jon said. "Just us three – we're going to free the French back to France. I hope you're not French. I'm Polish. I hate the French, I'm going to free them. Come on, Jason."

We saw them through the window, three of them, with loafers and tight jeans going towards the club. Tiki torches were burning by the lake.
"I'll free them," Jason said. "What are they doing in Palm Desert?"
"I'm going to stay here," Kelley said.
"I'll stay," Grey said.
"Oh, please don't!" Kelley said. "For the love of God please go somewhere. Can't you see that Jack and I want to talk?"
"Uh, no," Grey said. "I'm just pretty drunk so I thought I'd just sit here."
"Jesus, that's no reason to just go on sitting with someone. If you're drunk, go pass out somewhere. Go to bed. Go."

"Do you think he got the point?" Kelley asked. Grey was gone.

"Jesus! I'm over him!"

"He's not the life of the party, is he?"

"He's depressing."

"Damn depressing. And he's had every chance to be fun and happy."

"He's probably stalking the both of us right now."

"Yeah, he would. You know I think I know how he feels. He doesn't get it, though, that it meant nothing between us."

"Yeah right."

"Nobody else would be all depressing. I'm so over the whole thing. And Jonathan. Jonathan is awesome."

"It isn't a picnic for Jon either."

"Yeah, but he doesn't have to be such an ass."

"Everyone's depressing," I said. "Sooner or later."

"You wouldn't be so depressing." Kelley looked at me.

"I'd be worse than Grey," I said.

"I don't like it when we talk like that."

"OK, then, what do you want to talk about?"

"Don't go there. You know, you're the only person in the world that I can really talk to, and I fell depressed tonight."

"You have Jon."

"Yeah, and hasn't he been swell."

"Uh yeah," I said, "it's been lousy on Jon, having Grey around all the time and seeing you together."

"You're telling me? Let's not talk about it, it makes it seem worse than it already is."

Kelley was sort of shaking and I had never seen her nervous. She was smoking a cigarette, and looking into the distance, zoning out.

"Let's take a walk."

"Yeah, let's go."

I finished up my bottle of beer and threw it into the trashcan.

"Let's have another shot," Kelley said, "I need some booze."

We each had a shot of the smooth Patron silver tequila.

As we left the bar I saw Grey in the lounge across the way."

"He *was* stalking us," Kelley said.

"He can never leave your side."

"Poor bastard."

"He can't guilt trip me. I hate that guy."

"I hate his guts," she said, "I can't stand tip-toeing around his depressing passive aggressive ass."

We held hands and walked down the side of the hotel away from everyone and the lighted hotel rooms. It was dark outside and wet, and we walked over to the golf course by the waterways and through the mazes of quiet gardens and back around to the lights of the Italian restaurant. We could laughs and suddenly music."

"Want to check it out?"

"No."

We walked on the bridges over the waterways and saw the electric boats being driven through with the crowds of people. We found a bench behind some bushes by the water and we both sat down. Across the river by the golf course it was dark and wet from the dew and the wind was still. At our feet was the still water and you could see the moon reflecting.

"Don't sweat it, Kelley," I said.

"I feel like shit," Kelley said, "I don't want to talk about it."

    We look out at the water and the desert sky. The stars were all very bright and looked unlike the stars anywhere else in the world. The desert air was dry and hot in the night and you could feel your lips and throat dry when you breathed and Kelley stared straight ahead, ignoring the stars.
"I'm hot."
"Want to get back?"
"Through the pool."
    We got up and walked around towards the pool area back to the main hotel.
"Are you still in love with me, Jack?"
"Yes," I said.
"Because I've totally fallen," Kelley said.
"How's that?"
"I've fallen. I have it bad for the Barker kid. I think I'm in love with him."
"I wouldn't go there if I were you."
"There's no helping it. I've already fallen. It's tearing my guts out."
"Don't."
"I can't even help myself. It's never helped before, trying to help myself."
"You ought to help yourself."
She was smoking a cigarette. She was shaking.
"You can't stop your feelings, Jack. Look, I can't even stop this. Feel that?"
Her hand was shaking.
"That's how my whole body feels."
"Christ you shouldn't do it Kelley."
"Yeah, I know. But I can't do anything about it at this point. Isn't there a difference?"
"No."

"I just have to do it. It's something that I just can't not do at this point. Not like I have any self-respect left at this point anyhow."
"You don't *have* to do anything. If you want to do it..."
"Don't you start in, too Jack. How do you think it is for me to have that damn Grey around, and Jon the way he's been acting lately?"
"Um, yeah."
"I can't stay high all of the time, you know."
"Nope."
"Please just be with me tonight, Jack, I mean be my friend tonight and support me no matter what you think of what I'm doing."
"Yeah sure."
"I'm not saying that it's right or anything. But this is me, and I don't see anything wrong with it. I do feel like such a whore, though."
"What the hell do you want me to do?"
"Let's get out of here," Kelley said, "Let's go find him."
 We walked together back down the winding path thru the garden to the path that led back to the hotel.
Travis Barker was in the restaurant. He was at a table with other industry people. They were all talking loudly and drinking and having a good time. When we came in they all looked over at us. Barker smiled and nodded his head at us.
We sat at a table half way across the room.
"Go ask him to come over here."
"Let him come to you."
"I can't even look."
"He's alright to look at, you know."
"I've never cared what anyone else thought of me."
"Yeah, I know."

"I'm such a whore."
"Um, yeah."
"Jesus, the things a girl has to put up with."
"Yeah?"
"I'm such a whore."

     I looked over across the room. Travis raised his eyebrows and smiled over at us. He said some proprietary words to the large guys, probably bodyguards, and stood up. He came over to the table. I stood up to greet him and we shook hands.
"Would you like a drink?"
"You have to come over to my table," he said. He sat down asking Kelley if it was OK without even saying anything. She agreed. He was a very polite guy, not the rude or arrogant person that you'd expect of a rock star. He had great manners, and was very articulate. He was the kind of guy that after meeting him you would want to hang out with him again sometime. He lit up a cigarette.
"Marlboro lights?" I asked.
"Yeah, I only smoke these."

     It was illegal to smoke in bars and restaurants in California, but small allowances were made now and then in either very shabby places, or for special people. Somehow I didn't think the management here would tell him to put out his smoke. I caught him watching Kelley, and you could tell that he thought there was something there. He knew for sure when Kelley was holding his hand underneath the table. They were both being very careful and neither one of them wanted to make any mistakes.
"Are you playing tomorrow?" I said.
"Yes," he said. "It was raining today, and well, not like we wouldn't play if it was raining, but hopefully the weather will be nice."

"Did it?" I said, "rain?"
He nodded.
"Right here in the desert," he slapped his hand down onto the table. Kelley reached over and grabbed his hand, turning the palm up.
"Oh, you can read palms?"
"Yes. Want me to tell your fortune?"
"Sure. Tell me that I'm going to die young and rich."
He was very nice about Kelley and responded well to her, and now he was more confident and sure about what was going on between he and Kelley, "Hey," he said, "do you see anything about us in there?"
He smiled. His hands were big but not rough, and he had tattoos running down to his wrists on each arm.
"I see a thousand different girls here!"
"Oh no! You caught me. Tell me some more."
"There is a great deal of money here in this hand, unfortunately, it looks like he'll live for a long time."
"Tell my fortune to me, not your friend. Look at me."
"I said that you're going to live for a long time."
"I know it."
I wrapped my knuckles lightly on the table.
"No, no need for that. If I die young, I die rich and happy."
He was wearing a trucker hat and she pulled it around and down to this eyeballs.
"Don't die yet," Kelley said.
"No?"
"No."
"Sounds good to me."
He laughed.
"I want a hat like that."
"I'll see that my people get you one."

He took his hat off his head and put in on her, letting her try it out. He pushed it down so that the brim was down over her face and you couldn't see her eyes. Kelley was laughing.

"I think I'll go get you one of those for yourself."

I stood up. Barker rose, too.

"Stay," I said. "I've got to go find my friends."

He raised his eyebrows at me and we smiled as Kelley was pulling the hat off and there was an understanding between us. We understood all right.

"Sit," Kelley said. "You've got to show me your tattoos."

He pulled the chair over around to where Kelley was sitting and slouched down beside her. The industry people were giving me bad looks. When I cam back about a half hour later, Kelley and Travis Barker were gone. The beer bottles and our three empty seats sat in disarray. A waitress came over and picked up the bottles, wiped the table down and pushed the chairs in.

CHAPTER SEVENTEEN

Outside at the club I found Jason and Jon and Amanda. Amanda was the girl's name.
"They kicked us out," Amanda said.
"By security," Jon said. "There are some guys in there that you could say we didn't exactly *get along* with."
"I've been watching these two guys the whole night," Amanda said. "You've gotta help me out here buddy."
Jason's face was red.
"Go back on in, Amanda," Jason said, "go back in and dance with those guys."
"No way, you'll just get into another fight. Come on, they were just being nice."
"Those fucking assholes," Jason said.
"Come on," Jon said, "let's go in and kill those mother fuckers."
"Good old Jon," Jason said, "Let's go. These guys come here and they can't talk to us like that? We'll kill them."

"Those fucking jackholes," Jon said, "I'm going to kill those fucking jackals."
"They can't talk to Jon like that," Jason said. "This guy right here Jon is a good fucking man. They can't talk to him like that. Not if I have anything to say about it? I'm going to fucking kill them." His voice cracked.
"Do you want to know who cares?" Jon said. "I don't care. Jack doesn't care. Do *you* care?"
"No," Amanda said. "Did you really go to jail?"
"Of course. I went to federal prison. You don't mind, do you Jason?"

  Jason gave Jon a bear hug around his shoulders, not face to face, but from the side. He lifted Jon off of his feet.
"I wish it was me there in prison. I'd come visit you if you were in prison though. You're such a good forgetting guy."
"Those guys are assholes. Forget them, we'll go kick *them* out." Actually by that time the guys they were fighting with had simply left.
"The bastards," Jason said. "If I see them back here I'm going to go kill them."

  I think Jason had told them that his one weakness was that he liked to hurt people and that he'd crack open their skulls and stomp out their teeth or something.
"Do you know those guys?" I asked Amanda.
"No. It's the first time I've ever seen them. They thought they knew me."
"I was fine until they started in with the lip," Jason said.
"Come on, let's go back to the bar," I said.
"They're a bunch of twenty-one year old fucks that juice and lift weights and think that they own the fucking place. Fuck them," Jason said.

"They're just morons. You have to ignore them Jason. I'm going to get hit on, and you can't be so violent." Amanda said.
"I think one of them is John Carter, from Long Beach," Jason said.
Amanda started laughing and she couldn't stop.
"Let's get out of here," she said, "you bastards."
"How did the fight start?" I asked Amanda. We were walking up towards the main hotel lobby. Jason was gone.
"I'm not sure exactly, but someone called the police and had to keep Jon from going after the guys that were hitting on me. What's wrong with Jon?"
"It's probably that they said something that was somehow true," I said, "That's what usually gets to people."
In the lobby there were people waiting in line for the boats that will take you to the different restaurants. They were sitting on the marble planters and cushioned chairs that were in the area.
At the lobby bar we had just sat down and ordered beer when David Grey came up.
"Where's Kelley?" he asked.
"I have no idea."
"She was with you, right?"
"She probably went back to her room."
"She's not there."
"I have no idea where she is."
There were circles under his eyes that you could see in the dark. He was standing up.
"Tell me where she is Jack."
"Have a seat," I said, "Nobody knows where she is."
"Bullshit."
"You can shut your mouth."
"Tell me where the fuck she is."

"I'm not telling you anything."
"You know where she is."
"Even if I did know where she was I wouldn't tell you."
"Hey, what's your problem Grey," Jon shouted from the other table. "Kelley's hooking up with that rock star guy. They're in love."
"Shut up."
"Oh go fuck yourself," Jon said in a resigned manner.
"Is that true? Is that where she is right now?" Grey turned to me.
"Go fuck yourself."
"Tell me" – he came at me – "you fucking faggot."

I swung at him but missed. I saw his head move out of the way. He hit me and then I was sitting down on the floor. I was trying to get back up and he hit me a couple more times and I sort of fell down under a table. I had to get back on my feet but my legs weren't cooperating. I felt I could get him somehow. Jon helped me up. Somebody had a glass of water that they poured over my head. Jon had one arm around my shoulders and then I was sitting down in a chair. Jon was slapping at my cheeks.
"Hey, you were out," Jon said.
"Where were you?"
"Oh, different places."
"You didn't want to get in on the mix there buddy?"
"Jon was knocked out too," Amanda said.
"He didn't knock me out, I was just laying there."
"Does this kind of thing always happen to you guys?" Amanda asked.
"Wasn't that David Grey?"
"I'm OK. I'm OK. My head's a bit banged up."
There was a group of hotel guests and workers standing around.

"OK, move along. There's nothing for you to see here," Jon said.
The hotel workers ushered everyone out of the bar.
"It was something to see, you guys," Amanda said. "He must be a cop or something."
"He is."
"I wish Jason had been here," Amanda said. "It would have been interesting to see Jason knocked down. He's so big."
"I was hoping he would hit someone who worked here," Jon said, "He'd go to jail. I'd like to see his ass in jail the bastard."
"No," I said.
"Are you serious," said Amanda, "you don't mean that do you?"
"I do, I'm totally serious," Jon said, "I'm not one of these guys that likes to get punched in the face all the time."

Jon took a drink.
"I don't even like riding motorcycles or rock climbing or surfing. Too dangerous, you know? How are you doing Jack?"
"I'm all right."
"You're a good guy," Amanda said to Jon. "Did you really go to prison?"
"Absolutely."
"I was there for two years," Jon said. " Federal prison."
"That's why they call you a criminal isn't it."

I got up from the chair. Listening to them, hearing them, it was like they were talking from a long way away. Suddenly I felt that they were talking about me. It all seemed like some bad episode from a popular TV sitcom.
"I'm going back to my room," I said. I heard them talking about me.
"Is he O.K.?"

Let's walk with him.

"I'm O.K. Don't get up. I'll see you later."

I walked out and looked back at them and the empty bar. There was a bartender sitting with his head down at a table.

Walking across the hotel everything looked new. It was all different and new. I had never noticed the ferns. I had never seen the stucco on the walls. All at once, it was changed and all at once. It felt just like the time I came home from college for the weekend, driving in with my college girlfriend and noticing everything for the first time. Everything looked shabby and the people were all sad. Some people were hosing their driveway down and sweeping the water away. I had grown up on this street and lived here my whole life but I stopped and watched for a couple of minutes. It was very strange. Everything seemed like it was very far away and the sounds were coming from somewhere down the hall but around the corner or maybe through a funnel. I had a sinking feeling and it felt like it does sometimes before I'm going to be sick. That day coming home from college I had hit my head on the loft in my dorm room and I felt that way. It was like that walking thru the lobby. It took me a long time to walk down the hall and I felt like I was driving with my college girlfriend. The lights were on in the room. Jason came out and met me in the hall.

"Hey brother," he said, "Grey was asking for you. He got into some trouble and he wants to see you."

"Fuck him."

I didn't want to walk down another hall.

"What are you looking at?"

"I'm not looking at anything. Go up and see Grey. He's pretty messed up."

"You were pretty hammered back there," I said.
"I'm pretty hammered right now," he said, "but you go up and see Grey, he wants to see you."
"O.K," I said. It was just a matter of putting one foot in front of the other, going to the elevator, getting off and walking down another hall. I rode up the elevator with my imaginary college girlfriend. I walked down the hall to Grey's room. The door was open but I knocked.
"Who is it?"
"It's Baker."
"Jack, come in Jack."

I pushed the door open with my foot and my college girlfriend waited out in the hall. I went in and Grey was lying on the bed, it was completely dark in the room. He was lying with his face in a pillow.
"Hey brother."
"Don't call me brother."

I stood in the doorway. It felt just like the time I came home with my college girlfriend. I needed a soft bed and some sleep. A nice soft bed to sleep in and just a little nap.
"Is there a bathroom here?" I asked.

Grey was crying. He was lying there on the bed, with his face in a pillow crying. He had an academy t-shirt on. The kind he wore when he was a cop.
"I'm sorry Jack, please accept my apology."
"Apology, shit."
"Please let me apologize Jack."
"I wasn't thinking. You've got to see that."
"I understand that."
"You called me a fucking faggot."

Like I cared what he called me. All I wanted was a soft bed to lie down in and go to sleep. A deep soft bed and a deep deep sleep.
"I'm sorry. I'm so sorry, it's not true Jack. Please forget about that."
"O.K. man it's O.K."
He was crying. His shoulders were moving and his voice was high and shaking. He was just there in his shirt, his cop shirt.
"I'm taking off in the morning."
He was sobbing without making any noise.
"I just couldn't stand to see Kelley in that way. It's been a living hell for me Jack. Torture. When we met up out here she pretended that I didn't exist and that we were total strangers or something. I couldn't bare it Jack. We stayed here together for a couple of weeks. I'm sure you heard about that by now. I just couldn't stand to see her like that."
He just lay there on the bed.
"Well," I said, "I'm going to bed."
"You were my best friend Jack, and I loved Kelley so much."
"Well," I said, "see you later."
"What's the point? There's never any point is there."
"What?"
"All of it. Please say that you accept my apology, Jack."
"O.K.," I said, "It's O.K."
"I feel so bad. It's been so terrible for me, Jack. Jack not everybody can deal with things like you and Jon and Jason. It's all over for me, Jack. It's all over. I've lost my best friend and the girl I love."
"Well," I said, "I'll see you later. I have to go."

He turned his head to the side and looked at me. He sat up.

"See you later Jack," he said. "Come here."

I shook his hand and he wanted to hug me but I backed away. It was dark and I couldn't see his face.

"See you in the morning," I said.

"I'm going to leave in the morning."

"Oh yeah," I said.

I left the room and he came out after me.

"Are you O.K., Jack?"

"Yeah, I'm fine."

I couldn't find my room. After a couple of floors I finally found it. I went into the bathroom and turned on the hot water. When I got to the bed I found one of my shoes off. I looked around for it and looked all around the room but couldn't find it so I took the other one off and fell into bed.

I woke up with a bad headache and heard the noise of people walking down the hall, bumping into the walls on their way out. Then I remembered that I was supposed to take Jason's friend Amanda to see the concert this morning. I got dressed and took the elevator down and walked out into the warm morning. People were driving out to the polo fields, and hurrying into the venue to see the shows. I went down to the lobby bar to have a cup of coffee. The bartender told me that my friends had already left for the show.

"How many were in the group?"

"Two guys and girl."

I could deal with that. Jon and Jason had Amanda with them. She was worried that they would get drunk, pass out, and not make it out to the show on time this morning. That's why I was going to take her to the show. I finished my coffee and ran out with all of the other people to my car to drive over to the polo fields for the concert. I wasn't tired anymore. I just had the headache. Everything was clean and clear and it smelt like cut grass outside of the hotel.

    The stretch of grass and palm trees between the hotel and the desert was wet with the morning. There were cars all around the valet area that led out the long driveway, and it was the last part of the drive to Indio that I remember. Arriving and parking my car in the dusty parking lot and diving into the crowd to enter the main concert area, I knew that I was too late to get up close in the pit so I hung back to watch the commotion. I heard the drums start and the bass, and it was going fast. I was pushed against the metal of a chain fence. Between the stage and a makeshift fence the police were pushing the crowd back. They would try to jump up on stage and dive back into the crowd. People trotted around or ran in circles around in the very front. They jumped off of shoulders onto the crowd itself and floated around on top for a while and then fell back down, kicking someone in the head on the way down.

    There were many screams and shouts from the crowd and I was swept up in a wave of people, out of control for now. Shoulder to shoulder. Everyone was happy, just popping and jumping up and down, and sometimes it was frantic and people were scared and pushing hard to stay on their feet. I felt someone pulling my shirt from below and I helped her to her feet. There were so many people packed into the area in front of the stage that the mass got very thick and was moving slowly. There was a guy trying to climb up onto the stage and the

cops had their batons out and hit him back. The police were scared. There were people being pushed against the fence in front of the stage and it looked like the crowd just there was getting out of hand. There was a girl that disappeared down under the crowd up front, and you could see that both of her arms were down by her sides. The band had stopped playing and they were telling everyone to be cool and to let people up and to back off and that they wouldn't play until everyone was cool. The girl that had disappeared into the crowd lay face down, not moving, in the dirt. People jumped the fences, and I couldn't see the girl because there was a circle forming around her. There were shouts coming from the stage. You could hear from the shouting on the stage that it was something that was very wrong, the thing going on over there. Then the concert was over and everyone was leaving. Back at the hotel I dropped in at the bar in the lobby.
"Anything interesting happen at the show?"
"I was there but didn't see it all. A girl was trampled to death in the pit."
"What?"
"Yeah," I drew my finger across my throat.
"Dead? Trampled? At a concert?" He put down some of the glasses that he was washing and leaned up against the wall. "Trampled to death at a rock show, for fun? Am I missing something?"
"I'm not sure."
"I mean everyone was there to see the show and have a good time?"
"You're not a fan?"
"Me? What are these shows all about? Getting into the pit? Getting up close?" He got back up and went back to

washing his dishes. "Trampled to death. That's nice. At a concert. Sounds like fun to me."

He kept washing his dishes, shaking his head and raising his eyebrows and whistling.

A couple guys were walking in and I overheard them saying, "Dead. I can't believe it." The bartender called them over to verify my story. One of them nodded his head, "Yeah, she was killed." The bartender came back over to my table. "Did you hear that? Yeah, she's dead alright."

"Terrible thing."

"Yea terrible. Fun? Not in my book."

We finally read in the newspaper that the girl killed in the mosh pit was Jennifer Jameson, and that she came from Redondo Beach. We saw on the news that she was twenty-four years old and had a boyfriend, and no kids. She came to the concert every year and was a fan of the band that she came to see when she died. I saved the newspaper clippings and ticket stubs from that particular show and gave them to Jason, who consequently gave them to Kelley, who in a fit of manic cleaning stacked everything up along with some hotel stationary and several Marlboro light cigarettes, and finally deposited all into a drawer already containing the book or Mormon. These artifacts remained in the table that stood beside her bed in the Desert Springs Marriott Hotel, in Palm Desert for quite some time.

Back at the hotel, the valet was sitting in a chair inside the hotel where it was air-conditioned. He was there since last night, and you could tell that he was sleepy. He got up as I came in. Other people staying at the hotel walked in with me at the same time. They had been to the morning show at the polo field. They went to the elevators laughing. I followed them and rode up to my room. I kicked my shoes off and lay down on the bed. The drapes were open to the balcony and the sun came in. I didn't feel like sleeping. It was probably something like four in the morning when I finally fell asleep and the people in the hall woke me up at six with their laughing and banging against the walls. My face and neck were sore all over. Goddamn David Grey. I massaged the back of my neck and felt my jaw with my hand. That guy should have had his tantrum a long time ago, and then just left. I couldn't imagine Kelley with that guy. But here they were and he was sure that they'd end up together if he stuck around long enough. The whole last–man-standing tactic. There was someone knocking on the door.

Jon and Jason came in. They sat down on the bed.

"Jesus, that was some show," Jason said, "What a show."

"Hey, weren't you there?" Jon asked. "Jason, call room service for some beer."

"What a day," Jason said. His face was red and sweaty and he wiped it with his shirtsleeve.

"Jesus what a day. And here's Jack just kickin' it. Jack, Tyson's sparring partner."

"What happened up front?"

"Holy shit!" Jason said, "What happened, Jon?"

"These guys came at us," Jon said, "in the pit, so we sort of pushed back just a little bit and they went down."

"And the whole crowd pushed back and walked over them," Jason said.

"I heard the yelling and screaming."

"That was Amanda," Jason said.

"People just kept coming and kept coming."

"One guy did a stage dive and laded on top of us and we threw him off."

"About a dozen people went to the hospital," Jon said.

"Jesus what a day!" Jason said. "The fucking cops also kept arresting people for wanting to have fun."
"They stopped playing in the end," Jon said.
"It went on for about an hour or so."
"It was really more like fifteen minutes," Jon said.
"Oh shit," Jason said, "It seemed like two hours."
"Where the hell is the beer?" Jon asked.
"What happened to that Amanda?"
"We just dropped her off at her room. She went to bed."
"How did she like the pit?"
"She was actually pretty good about it. We told her it was always like that."
"She liked it," Jon said.
"She wanted us to get right down in front, too," Jason said.
"She likes it pretty rough."
"I said it wouldn't be fair to my employer," Jon said.
"What a day," Jason said. "Holy shit, and what a night!"
"How are you felling there, buddy? How's your jaw?"
"It fucking hurts," I said.
    Jason laughed.
"You should have kicked him or something."
"Oh, so you're the tough guy," Jon said. "He'd have layed you out, too. I never saw him coming. I think maybe I caught him out of the corner of my eye, and then all of a sudden I was just out there laying in the bushes and Jack is down under a table."
"What happened to him afterward?" I asked.
"There's the most special lady," Jason said. "The beer's finally here."
The lady came in and put the tray with the beer, ice, and glasses down on the table.

"Actually, I think we're going to need to double this order," Jon said, "Can you bring up another couple Heineken? Thanks."
"Where did he go after he knocked me out?" I asked Jason.
"Didn't you hear about that?" Jon was working on one of the beers with a bottle opener. He poured the beer into one of the glasses, leaving as little head as possible.
"*What*?" Jason asked.
"Oh yeah, he found Travis and Kelley in Travis' room and he fucked Travis up."
"No way."
"Oh yeah."
"Holy shit what a night." Jason said.
"He nearly killed Travis. Then Grey wanted Kelley to marry him. He insisted that she marry him. I'm sure it was all a goddamn gorgeous scene."
"He's a jackhole."
"What happened after that?"
"Kelley went off on him. She told him where to go in no uncertain terms, and knowing Kelley – probably did a good job of it, too."
"Um, yeah I bet she did," Jason said.
"The Grey was crying for her and begging for Travis to forgive him and to shake his hand. He wanted Kelley to shake on things too."
"Oh yeah, we shook hands that night."
"Did you? Well they weren't having any of it al all. Travis was a champ. He didn't say anything, but he kept trying to get at David Grey, and kept getting beat down. Grey couldn't lay him out. It really must have been gorgeous to watch."
"Where did you get all of this from?"
"Kelley. I saw her this morning."

"How did all of this end up?"

"Looks like Travis was sort of laying or sitting on the bed. He'd been beaten down about a dozen and a half times, but he still wanted to get Grey. Kelley got between the two of them and wouldn't let him get up anymore. He was eventually able to get by Kelley and Grey wanted to shake his hand but he wouldn't have any of that. Then Grey said he wouldn't hit him anymore. Said he just couldn't do it anymore. Said it would be mean. So Travis sort of limped over there toward him. Grey backed into a corner.

" 'You won't fucking hit me?'

'No man, please, I'm sorry let's call it quits.'

"So Travis hit him as hard as he could in the mouth, and then fell down to the floor. Then he couldn't move and Kelley was trying to get him on the bed. He did say that if Grey tried to help that he would kill him. And that if he saw Grey after this morning that he'd kill him. Grey was all in tears and sobbing and Brett told him to leave. I think I've starting to repeat myself."

"No, no, finish the story." Jason said.

"She said that Travis was there on the floor, and he was breathing hard and trying to get up the strength to take another shot at David Grey. Kelley wasn't going to give him a hug, though, or shake his hand, or anything and Grey was sobbing with tears trying to tell Kelley that they should be married and she was telling him not to be completely stupid. Then Grey leaned down to try to shake hands and to hug Travis and Travis hit him in the mouth again."

"That kid has some fight in him." Jason said.

"I think it totally surprised Grey," Jon said. "I think the last punch really got to him."

"Where was Kelley when you saw her this morning?"

"She came up to the room this morning to get her things. She's going to take care of Barker now."
He poured himself another beer.
"She's pretty shaken up over the whole thing, actually. She's always the rescuer. That's how we ended up together. She was rescuing *me*."
"Oh yeah, I know." I said.
"I'm pretty drunk," Jon said. "I think that I'm going to get even drunker. All of this is pretty damn hilarious, but it's not so funny. Not too funny to me, it isn't."
He finished his beer.
"I gave her a pretty decent telling off myself, you know. I said that if she would fuck cops and white trash, that she should expect these sorts of low things to happen, and do you know what she told me: 'Yeah, and I've had such a good time with you fucking yuppies.' "
"That was a good one. The last guy she was with, I think his name was Davis or something used to hold a gun to her head or something in bed and I think the guy she married couldn't actually clossa-the-deal if you know what I mean. She's had some pretty rough spots, Kelley. Too bad, too – she gets such a kick out of life."
He got up. His voice was shaking.
"I'm going back up to the room to get some sleep."
He winked.
"I haven't slept in a week. We go way too long without sleep. Who was it that said happiness is directly proportional to the amount of sleep you get? Anyhow, sleep makes you live longer."
"See you at breakfast down in the café."
Jon opened the door and walked out. We heard him crash down on his bed in the next room. He called room service.

"Can you bring up six Coronas and a bottle of tequila?" Jon asked.

"I'm going to crash," Jason said. "Poor guy. Kinda know how he feels, don't you?"

"Who, me?"

"Yeah, you know with Kelley and everything? Aren't you in love with her?"

"You know, that's what makes it so terrible. I couldn't care less."

"Well she shouldn't pull that kind of shit, you know?"

"Was anyone hurt down in the pit by you guys today?"

"I'm not sure. I don't think so."

"A girl was killed up front."

"Is that right?" said Jason.

CHAPTER EIGHTEEN

By about two o'clock we were all in the hotel café. It was packed. We ate breakfast, even though it was afternoon. Every table was full. People kept streaming by with luggage and bags, followed by valets and porters who work for the hotel. Everyone was checking out and heading over to the concert area. It was the last day of the concert.
The party went on and did not stall out. The constant flow of people out of the hotel did not pause. I imagined what it would be like at the polo field: as soon as people parked and got out of their cars, they were swallowed up in the crowd. You didn't see them as people, you just saw the colors of their red and yellow 50-holed doc martens, or their black fishnet stockings, or their purple mohock and black makeup, or their ripped up jeans jackets with Ramones patches sewed all over and "OBEY" written in Sharpie pen. All the time you could hear music playing

both from the concert venues and from people's cars. People were dancing and yelling and causing scenes as people formed circles around the most interesting things.

"Here comes Kelley," Jason said.

I looked over and saw her walk out of the elevator, coming down the hall, her chin up, as though she was the reason for this party, and she found all of the people and the fuss about getting down to the polo fields just slightly amusing.

"Hey you guys!" she said. "I'm *so* thirsty!"

"Another one of these bloody marys here," Jason said to the waitress passing by.

"Breakfast?"

"Is Grey gone?" Kelley asked.

"Yes," Jason said. "Took off this morning."

The bloody mary came. Kelley started to lift the glass to her lips but her hand was shaking so she quickly put the glass back down and used the straw to sip the drink. "Good."

"Very good," I said. I was worried about Jon. I'm not sure if he ever got to bed and you could smell the beer and tequila. He seemed all right for the moment.

"I heard David got you pretty bad, Jack."

"Not a scratch. Knocked me down, that's all."

"Hm, well he did actually do a number on Travis Barker," Kelley said, "He pretty much almost sent him to the hospital."

"How's he doing now?"

"He's going to be O.K."

"How does he look? Is he all messed up?"

"Yeah pretty much he left a mark. His face is all black and blue, and his lip – well it isn't pretty, let me just say that. It isn't pretty."

"Is he going to play?"
"Yep. I'm going to go watch with you guys, if you don't mind."
"So *how's* your new friend?" asked Jon. He hadn't listened to anything Kelley had just said. Or rather he heard, but just didn't listen.
"Kelley's with a rock star," he said. "She was with a cop named Grey, but that didn't turn out so well."
Kelley got up.
"I'm not going to take this kind of crap from you Jonathan."
How's your new lover?
"Fucking fine," Kelley said. "You'll see him this afternoon yourself."
"Kelley the rock star," Jon said. "Kelley the mother fucking star fucker."
"Can you come with me? Jack, you'll come with me, won't you?"
"You tell him all about fucking your new star," Jon said. "Oh fuck you and your fucking bullshit!" He slammed both of his fists down on the table and then tipped the table over and all of the breakfast crashed down onto the floor.
"Come on Jack," Kelley said, "Let's get out of here."
Walking past the onlookers I said: "There's nothing to see here, move along."
"So, Kelley…. I um, how's it going?"
"I'm not going back to his room after lunch. His manager and everyone at the radio station is pissed at me. They're blaming me for David Grey, he tells me."
Kelley was beautiful. The sun was hot and it was bright without sunglasses.
"I feel like a different woman," Kelley said. "You have no idea how it feels Jack."

"Can I do anything for you?"
"No, please just come with me to the show today."
"We'll see you at lunch, then."
"No, I'm going to eat with him in his room."

We were standing in the shade of the valet stand at the entrance to the hotel. There were people carrying chairs outside and setting them up out on the lawn.
"Want to walk over to the spa?" Kelley asked, "I don't want to go back to the room. I think he's asleep."

We walked on the path, around towards the pool and the shops, moving with the other people on the walkway. We could see a bunch of people heading for the pool, and we could cut through there to make our way to the spa.
"Let's not go this way, by the pool area," Kelley said, "I don't want to be seen anywhere right now."

We stood right out in the sun now. It was hot and dry after the moisture of the morning had burned off.
"I hope it cools down," Kelley said. "This heat is really bad."
"I hope it cools down, too."
"He says he'll be alright for the show."
"That's good."
"Is that the spa?"
Kelley looked over at the white walls of the spa.
"Let's go over to the bar," Jason said. "I need a beer."

It was the last date of Coachella. Outside it was still hot and dry. The parking lot was full of people and you could smell beer and dust and portable bathroom. Girls were wearing less and less clothing and guys were watching them.
"Where's Chris?" I asked Jason.
"I have no idea."

We watched the first few acts of the last night of Coachella. The beer we drank made everything seem better. I drank mine too slowly and by the time I was almost finished the last bit would be warm and I'd toss it out and go get a new one.
"I feel really bad about Grey," Jason said. "I'm not sure he had such a good time."
"That guy can go to hell," I said.
"Where do you think he went?"
"Back to the 909,"
"What do you think he's going to do?"
"Oh, to hell with that guy."
"Seriously, what do you think he's going to do?"
"Probably get back together with his ex."
"Who was his ex?"
"A girl named Rebecca."

We both had another beer and another shot. We were on our way back to the hotel and then we found ourselves at the hotel bar drinking martinis and more beer to follow these drinks.
"When do you go back?" I asked.
"Tomorrow. Yeah."

We both sat and watched people go by. After a couple of minutes Jason said: "Well, it was a good show, wasn't it."
"Yeah, pretty good."
"Almost unbelievable."
"Almost," I said. "Yeah."
"Hey, what's the matter, feeling depressed?"
"Depressed as hell," I said.
"Drink that," Jason said. "Down it."

The sun was setting. The music went on playing. I started to feel the drinks kick in but it didn't make me feel any better.

"There, feeling better?"

"I feel like shit."

"Another beer?"

"What's the point? I'll be a sad drunk."

"Have another shot there. It's good for you. Make you feel better. You never can tell if it's the first or the fifth that'll get the job done. Hey, another round for us over here!"

I sipped the beer and took another shot, sipped at the beer again at first and then I started gulping and I spilled a bit. I hope that it missed my shirt but didn't look down to see.

"How's that beer?"

"Good. The problem with me is that I'm always so thirsty."

"Good."

"You're supposed to shoot for the mouth, not the shirt there, buddy."

I put my pint down. I hadn't meant to spill it all over myself.

"I'm drunk."

"You sure did, there, buddy."

"Hey where you going?"

"I'm going back to the room."

I was as drunk as I had ever been. My ears were ringing and I could hear myself breathing. I went upstairs past Kelley's room and her door was propped open. I pushed my head in and saw Jon sitting on the bed. He waived me in with a bottle he had in his hand.

"Jack," he said, "Come in here Jack."

I went in and sat down on the bed. The room was sort of moving around until I fixed both of my hands on something stable. The bed.
"Kelley. She left with Travv. Travis."
"No."
"Hit this." I did.
"That girl. That ... girl, man. What the fuck is wrong with her?"
"I don't know man. That girl. Shit."
"Yeah."
"I'm fucked up, man. I'm going to go and crash."
"Are you faded? I'm totally faded."
"Oh yeah, I'm faded."
"That's tight," Jon said. "Go crash then Jack."
  I left the room and went back down to my own and fell down onto the bed. I was spinning backward through the mattress and I propped myself up on three or four pillows to stop the falling. Outside there were tons of people at the club and the party went on. It didn't mean anything to me. A couple of hours later Jason and Jon came in to get me to go eat with them. I was asleep.
"He was pretty messed up last night."
"Totally hammered. We'll get him later."
  I got out of bed and opened up the curtains to let some light in the room and went out onto the balcony where it was very hot and I had to squint my eyes from the sun and the heat. The room wasn't spinning anymore and I wasn't falling down through the bed. I went back in the room, splashed some water on my hair. Cleaned up. I looked strange in the mirror and I went down to join the group.
"Hey, Jack man! There you are. I knew you wouldn't crash forever."

"Hey you drinker," Jon said.
"I had to have some food so I woke up."
"Have some of this French toast here."
The three of us sat there and had breakfast together. It felt like a dozen people were missing.

PART THREE

CHAPTER NINETEEN

The next day Coachella was over. I woke up at six in the morning and I could still feel last night's drinks. I knew it was too early to wake up so I went back to sleep and got up some time after ten. I jumped in the shower, put my clothes on and walked down to the pool. Already it was too hot to be outside. There were some Mormon families getting ready for a full day of sunbathing, the women all in their one-piece bathing suits. I sat sideways on one of the lounge chats and waved to our favorite waitress. There were some concert flyers blowing by in the wind and my waitress finally made it over to them, casually picked them off the ground, crumpled them up, and threw them in the garbage can. The party was over.

    I drank some coffee and Jason came down from the room, and walked form the gate over to where I was sitting. He ordered an orange juice and sat down. "Damn, look's like the party's over," he said.

"When are you taking off?"
"I don't know. Want to drive back together?"
"Wish I could. I'm going to stick around for a couple of days and relax a bit."
"I need to get back to work. Need to get home."
"What's Jon up to?"
"He's flying back to San Francisco today."
"Let's give him a ride back to the airport."
"O.K. I'll have the valet bring the car around."

    We ate some lunch and I had them put the tab on my room. The car was waiting for us outside in the front, off to the right of the entrance. The valet had started the car and left the air conditioning running for us. The car's thermometer showed 114 degrees external temperature. We drove down the tall rows of palm trees on either side and made a right on country club to get to Bob Hope. It was a quick ride to the airport. Jon smoked a cigarette in the back and the cabin was instantly drained of cool air. There is a certain melancholy feeling about smoking cigarettes in a bone-dry blast oven heat. It was an oppressive sort of quiet, shrinking feeling. So we all smoked our Marlboro lights on the way to the Palm Springs airport and didn't say much until we arrived at our destination.
"My flight's not for another three hours."
"Let's stop for a drink."
"Where?"
"Let's go to that Mexican place downtown – down where they have the water misters. Let's get in out of this heat."

    We continued on downtown and found ourselves on Taquitz Canyon road.

    We stopped the car right in front of the place and I tossed the keys to the valet. We all sneered and blasphemed at the blast of heat we had to endure walking into the restaurant and sat on three tall chairs at the end of the bar.

"Everything in that car is going to melt."

"Let's have some margaritas."

"We'll each pick up one round."

When the first round of margaritas arrived they were mixed, not blended. Without salt. They served them from a large clear glass pitcher and the margaritas quenched our thirst and picked up our spirits. We ate tortilla chips with salsa and guacamole. The chips you got there were made out of finely ground corn and fried, or at least heated up each day. The salty chips and fresh, thick avocados were something that you couldn't get anywhere else in the world, at least not outside of Southern California or Mexico. Our conversation started to pick up after the nourishment of the chips and salsa, and the guacamole. We decided to split the next round of beers and tequila evenly amongst our credit cards.

"I'm sorry sir, we can't accept this card." It was Jon's card.

"I'm so sorry, I can't pay for the drinks. I'm broke."

"How's that?"

"My cards are all maxed, and my ATM has a negative balance. I spent everything."

"I had just enough to pay for my tab at the hotel. Barely enough."

"I'll float you a couple bucks – what are you going to do after this?"

"Some checks should be coming through. I have to collect on some business accounts that are over due."

"This one's on me," Jason said. "Does Kelley have any money?"

He raised his eyebrows at Jon.

"I sincerely doubt it. She gave me the couple grand I used to cover my tab at the hotel. All I have are my plane tickets."

"So she doesn't have anything on her? Credit cards?" I asked.

"I don't think she has anything. Actually, she's always broke -- if you can believe it. Her parents have her trust on hold until she finishes school."

"I thought those trusts are as good as gold."

"Yeah, right. The parents have all of the control. The parents just can't spend it themselves."

"Cheers, guys."

"Here's to the wonderful world of finance, and ignoring it for as long as humanly possible." I said.

"Here here," Jason said.

We all drank the rest of the margaritas on that happy note. After the margaritas, we had several more rounds on Jason.

"Let's get out of here."

"Anywhere in particular that you'd like to go to?" Jason asked.

"Anywhere. Let's drive up towards the mountain."

"There isn't anywhere to go up there in the mountains."

We ended up driving out towards the freeway. We saw yellow sand, rock, and mountain. It was very apparent how much water must have to be expended to provide the lush green landscaping of the country club gardens and golf courses. The desert was so dry and so bleak, and there is a great divergence in color where they start the water for grass, trees, and people. There was, however, always the great presence of San Jacinto, which gets a fair amount of snow each season, and San Gorgonio on the other side of the pass. We had to drive thru these gigantic features, thru a pass to reach our destination. We'd have to pass thru these again to get back home and nobody was welcoming

the drive. The road went on, up to the freeway and we turned back, not wanting to face the reality of going back home. Finally, we turned back around and took side streets all the way back to the Palm Springs airport. Jon got out of the car, went into the trunk to get his gear. He came back around and we all got out of the car.
"Hey it was nice seeing you guys. Thanks for the great party."
"Take care," Jason said.
"Until next time," I said. "I'll see you soon."
"Forget about that bar tab, by the way," Jason said.
"See you later Jon."
"See you guys. What a party."

We shook hands all around and I gave Jon a bear hug, slapping him hard on the back. We drove away and waved goodbye to Jon from the car. Jason was due back at the hotel, so we drove back up on Highway 111. I had my bags loaded in the trunk and I think Jason hadn't packed yet or checked out. I stopped at the valet stand one last time and got out of the car. I let the valet know that I was just dropping Jason off.
"Have a good drive home now," I said.
"You take care, buddy."
"See you later."
"Later." We shook on that. We hit each other's fists knuckle to knuckle.

I pulled out of the Marriott and continued up to the resort at La Quinta where I was planning on unwinding for a week or so before getting back to work. I pulled into the hotel and checked in at the front desk. They gave me a villa right next to a pool with a small patio with two chairs and a table outside. It was very much like a room I had rented in Italy. I wondered if this was an accident, changed my clothes, and walked to the mall area where some people were walking around and eating lunch.

In the gift shop I bought a *Los Angeles Times* and say outside with a latte to read it. It was very strange to be here alone, and in out in the desert. Somehow I was thinking that I should have gone back to Riverside with Jason, expect that it would have meant more partying. It would be quiet here, and that's what I felt I needed. I could hang out in this room, swim in the pool, eat, drink, and practice my Spanish with the maids. At night there would be people at the bar, and probably some live music or other entertainment going on.

"How's the restaurant?" I asked the concierge.

"Very, very good."

"Sounds good."

I made a reservation for later that night, went back to my room, changed into some nicer clothes, and finally made my way back to the main dining hall. I had a bottle of Silver Oak to keep me company. It was very good and it felt great to be eating and drinking alone. It was a very nice meal, and afterward I had an espresso. The waiter asked if I'd like to have a martini, and I asked him why would I want that after the espresso, and I think he was mad at this question.

I was dwelling on the fact that I may have been too rude to the waiter, and so I left him twenty dollars more than I should have for a tip, and thought about this as I was walking back to my villa. I'm sure he'd greet me with a smile when I returned to his section. He'd appreciate the good tip, and would be happy to see me again, even though I had insulted him. It's a strange thing about most Americans, and especially most American businesspeople – they don't mind an insult so long as they get paid. This is where I had always diverged from the norm. If someone insulted me, I would never give a damn if they paid or not, and when they did pay I felt the money was spoiled in some way and I resented them for messing up the relationship. But this waiter I'm sure would enjoy the twenty bucks at P.F. Changs or one of the local places and not think twice about the insult. I summarized this in my mind as "You get what you pay for."

The next day I started to execute faithfully on this concept and gave out more tips that I usually do. Everyone appreciated this, of course, and I started to receive many more smiles, and people happily greeted me by my last name. They called me "Mr. Baker," even though I'm in my mid-twenties and I've always looked young for my age.

After breakfast I smoked a cigarette, and took a nap. I felt foolish for handing out my money in tips, and didn't have a very good nap. I tried to focus on how good it felt to be inside an air-conditioned room on such a hot day. The desert can and often does get quite hot, and wherever you go the air conditioning is always going full blast, and the inside of my villa was no exception. Today was probably about 100 degrees outside, even at about eight in the morning it was nice to be inside an air-conditioned room. Many of the rooms in La Quinta are individual little villas that have a nice bathroom, nice cool tile floors, and a shaded sitting area outside where there are usually several chairs and a table for drinks.

Since I couldn't get to sleep, I rolled out of bed and started to get all of my gear straightened out. I took my hanging suitcase, unpacked it, and hung up in the closet. I took my notebook computer out of my black leather briefcase and set it up, and I had a roller with all of my papers, books, and other things, which I unpacked and stacked neatly on the desk. I turned my computer on and typed in the password needed to get it started up. I sat there and watched the entire boot process. I had to plug in my mouse and network card after the computer was completely booted, which took about five minutes. After my computer was on and logged into the network, I realized that I was hungry.

    I walked over past my swimming pool to the main office, said hello and asked the staff if I had any messages. None had arrived, so I walked over to the deli and had lunch.

    When I was done eating I walked back to my room, read the newspaper that I had bought back at the deli, and went right to sleep. When I woke up, I realized that I had been asleep for several hours and that it was about five o'clock. I put my board shorts on, my Reef sandals, and put my room key in the single front pocket of my bathing suit. The pocket was secured by sturdy ultra sticky Velcro, which I had trouble unsticking. As an afterthought I also grabbed two towels from my bathroom and I walked out to the swimming pool. Some laughing and splashing noises that woke me up from my nap inspired my haste. I wanted to get out to the pool as soon as possible. There were several people lying around the pool with drinks and in the pool itself. The smell of chlorine was very strong, but it smelled nice in the afternoon heat. I took my sandals off and the smooth cement burned the bottoms of my feet so I danced around while I looked for a place to put my things before I jumped into the pool. All of the Villas in this resort were arranged so that many of them shared a private feeling pool area, of which I was in one. I threw my towels down on the chair that was farthest away from anyone else, and went over to the side of the pool, jumping and dancing on the hot pavement. I jumped feet first into the pool and tried not to let my head go under the water. Once I had pulled that trick off, I decided to dive down and wet my

hair. I dove down, opening both of my eyes wide, closing them before I came back up. My hair was wet and slicked back against my head, and I had to wipe my eyes and blow my nose to be comfortable once I came back up to the surface. The water was lukewarm and not extremely refreshing so I swam around and splashed some kids that were playing in the pool and swam underwater for a while. After about two minutes I was bored with this and quickly went over to the side of the pool and got out with one motion, pushing myself up and out of the pool with my hands and arms without using the steps or a ladder. There were two girls at the pool who had much of the OC Newport Beach look about them. They looked to me like they were a part of a bachelorette or wedding party. I was stealing glances at them, and at one in particular I think we made eye contact about a dozen times. It didn't look like they were with anyone. I pretended to ignore them for the rest of the af
ternoon. The one I was ignoring undid her strap and rolled over to brown the other side. At that point I got up and this time jumped back into the pool making the biggest splash possible. I did two laps, quickly got out of the pool, grabbed my towels and walked right back to my room, which was no more than 20 ft away from the pool. Overall, I knew I had to do a good job of ignoring them in order to keep their interest for later that evening. After I took a shower and changed into some comfortable shorts, I went out onto the porch of the villa and read and smoked cigarettes for a while.

After a while it started to get dark and the girls that I was watching gathered up their things and left the pool without taking even one dip in the pool. I'm sure it was to keep their makeup intact, or for some such reason. I like it better when a girl actually goes swimming, but you could

THE 909

just tell about some girls that they would never go for a swim with you. There was a golf tournament going on, a PGA golf tournament and many of the golfers were stopping into the resort with their friends and managers. In the dining room there was a table of them that were paying pretty close attention to their food, but one table in particular looked like fun, so I asked for a seat close by. The golfers all drank beer and had excellent tans. They all looked like they took golf very seriously, which was sort of a joke to me – but you can't get on anyone's case for being good and excellent at golf, and you shouldn't hate Golf just because it's popular. That's how I felt about golf at the time. I felt sort of an amused indifference to the whole scene. For these guys here it's the only sport in the world. And a lifestyle, for that matter. Personally, I like the desert and I think it has more to offer than just golf. For instance the San Jacintos and lesser groups of desert mountains are very beautiful, and I liked the climate. I don't need to like golf to like the desert like some people do.

I struck up a conversation with one of the professional golfers out on the patio after dinner while I was smoking and drinking espresso. The wind had been bad for the tournament, and also the dust was terrible for them. There were many new housing and business construction sites near La Quinta, which kick up dust. The city was trying to do what they could by making the builders water down their construction sites, but there was much wind and it kicked up the dust and it gave the professional golfers something to blame their performances on. He asked me if I was a fan and I told him that I play sometimes but don't follow the professional tournaments. He said it was the oldest and best sport and the most important sport in the world for business. I was sure that he was 100% right about that at the time, but now I'm not so sure. I think golf is pretty important for business, but if you could find another way to come up with an excuse to have a several hour conversation with someone, that would work just as well. Was I a part of the tournament he asked again. He asked me if I was a fan, probably to find out if I knew who he was. He said we should play together sometime. He asked me to come out and watch the game tomorrow and they get started way too early, but I told him that I'd see him there anyhow. The two girls by the pool came out onto the patio area, obviously to see about talking with us, the one I had been exchanging glances with earlier said hello to me. Was she baiting the gofer? I didn't think so because her friend was staring at the golfer. I'll be damned if his wedding ring didn't disappear in about two seconds.

Early the next morning I woke up and heard people leaving the villas next door, probably leaving for the golf tournament. I couldn't get back to sleep so I had coffee and read the newspaper before I got dressed to go for a swim. There was nobody by the pool so I dove in and swam the length of the pool underwater, coming up slowly at the other end of the pool. It was an easy length, and I came up very slowly and as quietly as I could. The water was somehow nice and cool and it felt good to be underwater and it felt nice to be absolutely quiet under the water. I floated around in the pool looking up at the blue sky, the palm trees, and felt the early morning sun on my face. The water in the pool was almost completely still and now I was lying with my body completely underwater, enjoying and relaxing and not wanting to move. After a while I got out of the pool and sat with some of the other people that started to do their sunbathing. When I was completely dried out by the sun I wandered back into my

Villa to check my email and see what was going on in the world.

I flipped up the monitor on my notebook and started Microsoft Outlook. There were about 5 messages in a row just coming in from Kelley. The first one read:

> CAN YOU COME TO THE ST. REGIS IN LAGUNA BEACH I'M IN BIG TROUBLE. KELLEY.

The second and third messages:

> CAN YOU COME TO THE ST. REGIS IN LAGUNA BEACH I'M IN BIG TROUBLE. KELLEY.
>
> CAN YOU COME TO THE ST. REGIS IN LAGUNA BEACH I'M IN BIG TROUBLE. KELLEY.

"O.K., I get it lady." I said to nobody. This meant that my stay at La Quinta had just ended, and I guess I had thought to myself that somehow something like this was going to happen.

I responded to her first email and said:

> WILL BE THERE TONIGHT LOVE JACK.

I didn't want to go into any detail, and I'm sure she'd get the message and I'm sure I'd be the only one coming to her rescue. How swell. Introduce her to a rock star, and go pick her up and bail her out of whatever trouble she got herself into. And I signed my email, "Love." Yes, she got the message all right.

I wasn't able to pack my things very well, and my suitcases were jammed and my car was a mess as I headed back down to the 10 freeway for my 4-hour car journey to save Kelley. I stopped at Hadley's and I watched the sun setting down over the power generating windmills. I couldn't care less about the windmills or the San Jacinto or Riverside. The 10 freeway to the 60 to the 91 to the toll road and down the 5 leads you to Crown Valley Parkway, which is the end of the line as far as a trip of this magnitude is concerned. After following Crown Valley up and around and making a couple of turns you arrive at the St. Regis at Monarch Bay.

"I need to see a guest, one Kelley Taylor."

The receptionist looked at me with recognition, I had been here before. She got some information from her computer and gave me the room number. Kelley must have left my name somehow with the reception because they would never give out room numbers without express permission from their guests.

"Muchas gracias," I said.

"No problem," she replied.

"Would you like a room here, Mr. Baker?"

I hadn't decided yet, but I'd let her know just as soon as I found out about my plans, thank you very much. The lady mentioned Kelley's room number again and I went on my way to the room. Her room door had been propped open somehow. Upon closer inspection, she had used the deadbolt to keep the door from closing completely.

I knocked three times before walking into her room, which smelled of her.

"Hello there?" Kelley said, "Jack?"

"It's Jack alright."

"Oh thank God, please come in."

I was already in the room, but I kept walking towards the bed and I went over to her and gave her a big hug. Then we were on the bed kissing each other, but I could tell that she wasn't into it. She was sort of shaking in my arms and she felt very small and diminished.
"Baby, I had such a terrible week."
"Tell me more."
"Well there's nothing much really to say. He took off yesterday. I made him leave."
"You didn't want him around?"
"I'm not sure. I don't know."
"Well I'm sure he was happy to play honeymoon."
"He shouldn't be married to anyone, that's for sure. I could tell you that the second I met him."
"No way. What do you mean?"
"Oh shit, can we talk about something else? I never want to talk about it again."
"O.K."
"It was like in some way he was ashamed to be with me. Seriously, can you believe that? *Him* ashamed of *me*?"
"What?"
"Oh yeah, he would totally not even want to be seen with me in public. We didn't leave this room."
"Crazy."
"I didn't know whether I should try to keep him around or if I should tell him to get lost, or what. He offered to take me along with him to Japan."
"No way."
"I don't want to talk about this anymore. Can we not talk about it? Hey can I bum a smoke?"
"He taught himself to play the drums."
"I've heard."
"He proposed to me, you know."

"Oh yeah?"

"Yes, well, I can't even consider marrying Jon now."

"Maybe he thought he would get some of your class and style by marring you."

"No, it wasn't that at all. He really wanted us to live together and to be together. So I couldn't leave him and go off. He was really a jealous type, believe me."

"Well that must feel good for you."

"Yes, it does feel good to be wanted. Everyone needs to feel attractive and desirable. It feels good to be desirable to someone like him."

"Good for you."

"You know I would have went with him to Japan if I didn't think it would be bad for his career. We actually had some good times."

"Outside of how different you two are as actual people."

"Oh, yeah, he would have gotten used to talking with me. Well, he was too young for me, anyhow. I need someone that is at least 10 years older than me. I'm not one of these chicks that goes around dating younger guys."

"Good for you."

"And I do feel attractive and desirable and I feel like I get lots of attention from men, and I'll be just fine. I've never had any problem attracting men."

"That's good."

She turned her head away and I think she was looking for another smoke. But I felt something wet on my arm and I realized that the tears had come without any sobbing and that she was crying. I held her and now she started to shake and to talk to me and sniff and sob and cry. She wouldn't make eye contact with me. She kept crying.

"Let's not ever talk about him again, please not ever."

"Oh Kelley."

THE 909

"I'm going back to Jon." She was still crying and I held her close and I could taste the tears on her lips and cheeks.
"I'm going back to Jon, Jack." I could feel her shaking more now.
She still wouldn't look me in the eye. I played with her hair, smoothing it down over the top of her head. It was thin and fine and blonde and slightly wet from her tears.
"I'm not going to be one of those whores, Jack, and I don't want to talk about it ever again."
    We packed up and left her room at the St. Regis. I paid the bill.
"Oh my god, you're so good to me," she said. And that was that.
We took my car down to the Ritz, which is where I like to stay when I'm in The OC. I arranged to stay a couple of nights so that we could unwind from the whole ordeal.
"The best part about the bar here is the view, and the service here is absolutely amazing," I said.
"The Ritz is the only place where you can get any service these days."
"Actually, the I think the folks here are a bit stuffy, but the view is nice."
    We toasted the two drinks that were waiting for us at the bar. The drinks were good and we started to feel them right away. Outside you could see a nice break forming up and some guys riding.
"We'll have two more martinis, please."
"Coming right up," he said to us.
    The guy behind the bar brought us the second round of drinks, and left us as to be far enough away not to hear our conversation.
"This is a nice bar," Kelley said.
"Oh, yeah, though not quite as nice as the one in Paris. Remember that time in Paris in the bar down there?"

"I wish you wouldn't bring that up."
"And that other place?"
"You're feeling your drinks, aren't you, Jack?"
"They're really good, aren't they?"
"Yes, they are. Hey, did I tell you that he was only with 5 girls before me?"
"He must have only counted the ones that were his girlfriends."
"Oh Jesus, Jack."
"Well and he's got a long career ahead of him, you know."
"Oh, I don't know. I don't think he's that kind of a guy."
"Well, you're number six, then."
"Yes, that's me alright. Just call me Six."
"Doesn't that mean sex in Latin?"
"I thought we weren't ever going to talk about this."
"OK, let's change the subject."
"I just can't help it, Jack."
"I thought you said that you never ever wanted to talk about it, not ever. You're going to crack up if you keep on talking about him."
"I just can't help it."
"Why don't you give it a try?"
"You know I do feel good about not being a whore, Jack."
"Yeah, I'm sure."
"Some people have their religion, and their church, this is what I have now."
"Lots of folks have that, you know. There's nothing wrong with going to church. A little church never hurt anyone you know."
"Yeah right – nobody expects the Spanish Inquisition, you know."
    We laughed.

"Well, Jack, deciding not to sleep around is sort of like my new religion. God just never worked for me, Jack, and that's all I've got to say about that."
"Let's have another round, why don't me."

The bartender brought around two more martinis and left the shakers, which I guessed were made out of real silver. He brought out two new chilled glasses for us. We moved over to the dining room for lunch. It's actually one of the best restaurants around. Kelley ordered but didn't eat very much. She never does.
"How are you feeling there, Jack?" Kelley asked me. "God you can eat."
"Feeling good. Want an espresso?"
"Ugh, no thanks that's gross."

We walked outside so that Kelley could smoke.
"You like to eat, don't you, Jack?"
"It's one of the best things in life I can think of to do. I like to do lots of things, though."
"Like what? What things would you like to do?"
"You know, things. Stuff. Do you want an espresso, Kelley?"
"You already asked me once."
"Yeah, um, let's have another bottle of wine. What do you say?"
"That sounds just GREAT."
"I'm not that drunk yet," I said. How about you?"
"Don't get drunk on me Jack, I'm fine," Kelley said.

I think we had about two bottles of wine after our lunch there.
"Finish off that bottle, Kelley."
"Almost done," she said.
"Want to go for a drive thru town?" I said.
"Sure, I'd love to drive down the coast."
"I'll finish this bottle here and then we'll go for a drive."

We went up to the concierge asking for my car to be brought around so that I could drive it down the coast. I think it was a little obvious that I shouldn't be driving, but I didn't think about it at the time.

Outside we met the valet who didn't have my car ready like I'd asked, but rather a house car was waiting for us that would take us anywhere in town we wanted to go. It was a Bently I think. We got in the back seat and I asked the drive to take us to watch the grunion run down in San Clemente. The driver started the car, a barely perceptible event, and we started moving of the property and down the hill to The Pacific Coast Highway.
"Jack," Kelley said, "You're so good to me, Jack, wouldn't it have been great if we had ended up together?"

Up ahead a cop had pulled someone over and was giving a field sobriety test on the shoulder. Traffic slowed and Kelley put her hand on my arm.
"Sure," I said.

THE END

ABOUT THE AUTHOR

Jim Stewart currently resides in the 909. *The 909* is his debut novel. The majority of *The 909* was written on a three-month tour of Europe during the summer of 2002. Mr. Stewart has lived and worked in the 909 and abroad as an information technology consultant

www.ingramcontent.com/pod-product-compliance
Lightning Source LLC
LaVergne TN
LVHW041613070426
835507LV00008B/211